13 & COUNTiNG:
Rescue Me?

○ ○ ○ ○ ○ ○ ○ **Engaging Activities to Teach and Promote Problem-solving and Perseverance**

by
TAMARA ZENTIC, M.S.

BOYS TOWN
Press ®

Boys Town, Nebraska

13 & Counting: Rescue Me?
Copyright © 2016 by Father Flanagan's Boys' Home

ISBN 978-1-944882-00-6

Published by Boys Town Press
14100 Crawford St.
Boys Town, Nebraska 68010

Printed in the United States
10 9 8 7 6 5 4 3 2 1

**For a Boys Town Press catalog, call 1-800-282-6657
or visit our website: BoysTownPress.org**

Boys Town Press is the publishing division of Boys Town, a national organization serving children and families.

Table of Contents

Why Teach Students to Problem-Solve?

Students sabotage their chances of academic success by allowing toxic, negative thinking to take place. Problems and difficulties seem insurmountable to many. Youth need problem-solving skills that will help propel them in the next phase of their lives. Teaching students how to view problems as opportunities through multiple problem-solving strategies is critical in fostering healthier self-esteem and independence in our youth. This book is meant to offer strategies and activities that inspire youth to develop better problem-solving skills, gain more autonomy in the decisions they make, and cultivate an optimistic outlook on life's problems, stresses, and difficult situations.

The *Rescue Me?* lessons are coupled with the Boys Town Education Model®, which promotes the use of life skills and behavior training through the implementation of the Boys Town Social Skills. The lessons also invite and encourage the use of Executive Function Processes as part of the teaching emphasis. Executive Function Processes include those qualities such as zest, grit, curiosity, social intelligence, and self-control, to name a few.

Keeping in mind the developmental level of 5th-12th grade students, *Rescue Me?* provides easy to implement, effective, strategies to foster effective problem-solving abilities in students. The lessons are time effective, relational, and get to the heart of the issues. They give youth the opportunity to cultivate better practices for confronting and overcoming problems they face on a daily basis. Furthermore, an emphasis has been placed on incorporating the use of technology, through various devices, into the lessons, to better engage and motivate the students of the digital, 21st century.

Benefits of teaching *Rescue Me?*

- It's a great way to incorporate the Boys Town Social Skills into a topic that affects each one of your students.
- The activities are developmentally appropriate for 5th-12th graders.
- The lessons elicit thought-provoking discussions and self-examination.

- The activities are easy to use and don't require a large amount of prep time.
- Technology is widely used to engage and motivate students.
- This book can be used in numerous settings such as the classroom, homeroom, advisement, enrichment, interventions, and character programs.

How to Use this Activity Book

Using the activities and lessons in *Rescue Me?* is a great way to learn about and explore problem-solving skills and strategies that can help overcome negative thought processes, cultivate more positive behaviors, and develop life-long critical thinking abilities that will help students focus on the opportunities instead of "drowning" under the weight of their problems. The lessons have been structured in such a way that they can be taught in a class period, or can be extended and approached in ways that spread the lesson out over two or three class times. Some of this will be dependent upon the amount of discussion that is generated in the classroom.

Each activity provides a Materials List and step-by-step Instructions on how to deliver the lessons; while leaving room to tailor the activities for each class of unique learners and the issues they face. The Boys Town Social Skills are interwoven throughout the lessons and activities, as well as Executive Function Objectives. There are also suggestions for how to deliver the content in a "flipped classroom" approach. Detailed, teacher-friendly instructions are written in order to help teachers feel at ease when implementing the lessons that require a broader use of technology. Lastly, because helping teachers to conserve time is a priority, additional resources are listed, along with suggested answers to discussion questions.

Introduction

The inner tube was floating in the middle of my neighbor's pool. I was six at the time. The neighbor's daughter had gone inside, leaving three of us around the pool. My friend really wanted the inner tube. I had a swimsuit on, so she pushed me in the water to get it, completely unaware of the fact that I could NOT swim. My only recollection was my head going under the water. Fortunately for me, my friend realized I was going under and ran to get the 19-year old girl who lived there. Someone threw me a life preserver as she jumped in and rescued me. I had almost drowned.

Many of you have a similar story of absolutely needing to be rescued at a particular point in your life. It might have been a physical type of rescue, such as the one above, or it might have been a mental, emotional, or spiritual type of rescue. Individuals have been rescued from abuse, neglect, physical dangers and other life emergencies. These types of rescues are necessary. They are good. They can literally save our life, but are all of life's problems and difficulties in need of a lifesaving rescue?

Take for instance the butterfly. A butterfly is a beautiful insect that majestically flutters from flower to flower with brilliance and ease. The butterfly looks like it has never had to endure a hardship of any kind as it freely goes about its way. Yet, this is not the case at all. The butterfly starts out as a caterpillar that grows really fast. In fact, it grows so fast that it must go through a process called molting whereby the caterpillar must shed its present skin and get new skin. This can happen more than once. When the caterpillar is done growing, it then spins itself into a chrysalis, or a very small, hard, enclosed space that hangs from a tree or leaf. The caterpillar spends days, weeks, and sometimes even months inside this chrysalis resting and morphing into a completely different form. It goes through a complete metamorphosis and eventually becomes a butterfly. When the transformation is complete, the butterfly has another hard task to complete. This crucial, difficult task is breaking out of the chrysalis. The butterfly struggles to slowly free itself of the chrysalis. As it emerges, the wings are crumpled and wet and not ready for flying. The butterfly still clings to the chrysalis because the chrysalis is providing the fluid that is being pumped through its body and wings to make them bigger and fit for flying. Without this crucial stage, the butterfly's wings would not fully develop; therefore making it unable to fly.

Imagine for a moment you see a beautiful butterfly painfully struggling day after day to break free of its chrysalis, and out of compassion you want to do something to help it. So, you decide to help the butterfly out of its chrysalis. You want to "rescue" the butterfly from its struggle. You carefully help the butterfly out by snipping the chrysalis or tugging gently on the butterfly to set it free from its struggle. But instead of watching the butterfly flutter away, it hobbles around. You notice that the wings are underdeveloped and the butterfly is not capable of flying. It can no longer fulfill its purpose. You have rescued the butterfly, but at what expense? The butterfly is now doomed to a life of despair and helplessness.

The butterfly must struggle in order to be adequately prepared for the next stage of its existence. The struggle is what allows the fluid to pump throughout the body and the wings making them fit for flight. This necessary struggle becomes valuable.

Somewhere along the line, we have confused lifesaving rescues with butterfly "rescues." When a child is younger, it is important to protect him or her from dangers. But as the child grows and matures, we still give into his or her pleas for help and come to the "rescue." It's hard to watch someone, especially a child, struggle. We fail to see that struggles and failures can be a very valuable teacher for our youth. Difficulties and hardships teach our children about resiliency, grit, and success.

When we help students escape the hardships, challenges, and failures that confront them, we are interrupting the acquisition of the problem-solving skills they are going to need to propel them in the next phase of their life. By rescuing, we unknowingly take away a youth's ability to gain autonomy in decision-making and to flourish as the individual he or she was created to be.

As educators, parents, and youth workers, we need to offer numerous strategies and resources to students as they struggle through problems and hardships inside and outside of the classroom. We need to encourage them to keep trying and come alongside of them when they are wavering; yet stop ourselves from helping them out of the "chrysalis" too soon, and save the "rescuing" for real life, safety-threatening circumstances.

Defining and Adjusting

Have we confused lifesaving rescues with everyday rescues from hardships, failures, and difficulties? For many, the belief is we have. There are times in life when we need to accept a life preserver from someone, but there are more times when we can work it out on our own or with minimal assistance.

Students may feel like they need to be rescued from work that becomes too difficult or takes longer to complete, but instead of rescuing them, we need to be teaching them life strategies they can use to overcome their problems and gain autonomy in their abilities. Helping students shift their focus from only seeing the problems towards seeing the opportunities that surround them is a necessary step to overcoming the desire to be rescued. We want to encourage independence. The negative in life is easy to find so it is important we help students develop healthier, more positive ways of viewing their life situation and problems.

Activities included in this section are:
- **Defining Rescue**
- **Do You Want to Be Rescued?**
- **Recognizing the Signs**
- **Attitude Adjustment, Seeing Problems as Opportunities**
- **Mountains of Problems or Not?**

Defining Rescue

OBJECTIVES:

Social Skills: Students will contribute to group activities and discussions. Students will also practice how to share personal experiences.

Executive Functions: Students will show self-control by listening without interrupting, and curiosity by asking and answering questions to deepen understanding.

MATERIALS NEEDED:

- Lifesaving Rescue Story
- Butterfly "Rescue" Story
- "Rescues Compare and Contrast" worksheet
- Paper
- Pencil
- Boys Town Social Skill poster, "Sharing Personal Experiences"
- Boys Town Social Skill poster, "Contributing to a Discussion"

TEACHER INSTRUCTIONS:

1. Pass out the "Rescues Compare and Contrast" worksheet to students.

2. Explain that you will be reading two "rescue" stories to students. Tell them to record how they are alike or different on the "Rescues Compare and Contrast" worksheet.

3. Read the two different rescue story scenarios to the class. One is a rescue performed on someone who was drowning. (Lifesaving type of rescue.) The other is rescuing a butterfly that is trying to get out of the chrysalis. (This rescue harms the butterfly.)

4. Debrief with students. Explain that next they will be asked to share personal examples of rescues they have experienced, or know about, that are similar to the drowning rescue.

5. Remind students you expect them to share their examples appropriately by following the steps of the Boys Town Social Skill **Sharing Personal Experiences**:
   a. *Decide if you should share personal experiences with other people.*
   b. *Determine whether the person appears comfortable with what you are telling him or her.*
   c. *Share experiences that are appropriate for another person to know.*
   d. *If what you told the other person is confidential, make sure he or she knows that.*

6. After sharing the stories, lead a discussion about the possible danger involved when a lifesaving rescue is needed. Ask students to share their feelings about this, and record the feelings students have had after this type of rescue on the board.

7. Remind students of the steps of the Boys Town Social Skill **Contributing to a Discussion**:
   a. *Look at the person who is talking and wait for a point when no one else is talking.*
   b. *Make a short, appropriate comment relating to the topic being discussed.*
   c. *Choose words that are not offensive or confusing to others.*
   d. *Give other people a chance to participate.*

8. Encourage students to share examples of rescues they have experienced, or know about, that are similar to the butterfly story. (Example: They were working really hard on a math problem but someone else gave them the answer right before they got it on their own.) Ask: Did this type of rescue make them feel the same as a lifesaving type of rescue? If not, what was the difference?

9. On a piece of paper, instruct students to record whether they prefer to be rescued like the butterfly even when they don't need it, or if they prefer to solve issues on their own. Ask them to explain their answers.

   Relate this to the butterfly story. The butterfly was actually helped at first but ended up being harmed. How is this similar to what can happen to them? Ask for examples and discuss.

10. Break into groups of three or four.

11. Instruct students to, in their groups, brainstorm ways that the two examples of rescue stories relate to school. They should answer the following questions while they brainstorm:
    a. Do they always need to be rescued?
    b. Should they rescue others? Why or why not? Explain.
    c. Is there a difference between helping and rescuing someone? If so, what is the difference?
    d. When is it okay to rescue someone?

12. Ask each group of students to summarize the two different types of rescues and develop three of their own questions to further clarify the two. Share and discuss with the class.

Be ready to share a rescue
story of your own.

FLIPPED CLASSROOM:

Ask students to research and summarize the lifecycle of a butterfly. Instruct them to discover what would happen to the butterfly if it were helped out of the chrysalis early. Discuss the answers in class..

ADDITIONAL RESOURCES:

Online examples of rescues.

Lifesaving Rescue (Near Drowning) ○○○○○○

The inner tube was floating in the middle of my neighbor's pool. I was six at the time. The neighbor's daughter had gone inside, leaving three of us around the pool. My friend really wanted the inner tube. I had a swimsuit on, so she pushed me in the water to go get it, completely unaware of the fact that I could NOT swim. My only recollection was my head going under the water. Fortunately for me, my friend realized I was going under and ran to get the 19-year old girl who lived there. Someone threw me a life preserver as she jumped in and rescued me. I had almost drowned.

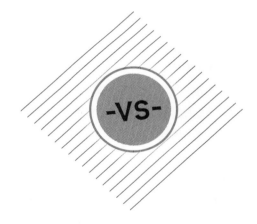

Butterfly Rescue

See next page for story.

○●○●○○○●○●○○○○○●○○○○○●●●●●○○

Butterfly Rescue

A butterfly is a beautiful insect that majestically flutters from flower to flower with brilliance and ease. The butterfly starts out as a caterpillar that grows quickly. In fact, it grows so fast that it must go through a process called molting whereby the caterpillar must shed its present skin and get new skin. This can happen more than once. When the caterpillar is done growing, it then spins itself into a chrysalis, or a very small, hard, enclosed space that hangs from a tree or leaf. The caterpillar spends days, weeks, and sometimes even months inside this chrysalis resting and morphing into a completely different form. It goes through a complete metamorphosis and eventually becomes a butterfly. When the transformation is complete, the butterfly has another hard task to complete. This crucial, difficult task is breaking out of the chrysalis. The butterfly struggles to slowly free itself of the chrysalis and when it finally emerges, the wings are still crumpled and wet and not ready for flying. The butterfly clings to the chrysalis because the chrysalis is providing the fluid that is being pumped through the butterfly's body and wings to make them bigger and ready for flying.

So, imagine for a moment you see a beautiful butterfly painfully struggling day after day to break free of its chrysalis and out of compassion you want to do something to help it. So, you decide to help the butterfly out of its chrysalis. You want to "rescue" the butterfly from its struggle. You carefully help the butterfly out by snipping the chrysalis or tugging gently on the butterfly to set it free from its struggle, but instead of watching the butterfly flutter away, you notice that the wings are underdeveloped and the butterfly is not capable of flying. You have cut off the source of the fluid that will help it to fly. Without this crucial struggle, the butterfly's wings cannot fully develop; therefore making it unable to fly. You have rescued the butterfly, but at what expense?

Rescues Compare and Contrast

DIRECTIONS: After hearing both stories, compare and contrast the two types of rescues.

Butterfly Rescue

- Isn't a life or death situation.
- Feel sorry for them.
- Harms the butterfly.
- The struggle is necessary for survival.
- Does not require quick action or a reaction.

Similarities

- Both appear to need help.
- Requires a judgment to be made.
- Need to access the situation.
- Intentions are good.

Lifesaving Rescue (Near Drowning)

- Usually a life or death situation.
- Usually an emergency.
- Requires quick action.
- Helps the person in need.
- Their rescue is necessary for survival.
- Don't have time to feel sorry for them.
- Spontaneous.

Do You Want to be "Rescued"?

OBJECTIVES:

Social Skills: Students will be able to identify their feelings about being rescued and will respond to others' feelings appropriately.

Executive Functions: Students will display social intelligence by demonstrating respect for the feelings of others.

MATERIALS NEEDED:

- Chart paper (at least 5 large pages)
- Masking tape
- Markers or other writing utensils
- Boys Town Social Skill poster, "Identifying Own Feelings"
- Boys Town Social Skill poster, "Responding to the Feelings of Others"

 Some students may be more sensitive than others about being "rescued" in their daily activities. Make sure the students cultivate an atmosphere of concern and respect so that all students will feel comfortable sharing.

TEACHER INSTRUCTIONS:

1. **Prior to class,** label five pieces of chart paper with the following categories:
    a. Obstacles I face.
    b. What's good about being "rescued"?
    c. What's bad about being "rescued"?
    d. Why do I feel the need or want to be "rescued"?
    e. How could someone help you without "rescuing" you?

2. Hang these in five different locations in the classroom.

3. **During class,** instruct the students they will be taking five minutes at each station and writing down as many ideas as they have for each category on the chart paper.

4. Explain to students this activity will require them to identify their own feelings about the topic and questions. They can practice the Boys Town Social Skill **Identifying Own Feelings** by:
    a. *Examining how they are currently feeling.*
    b. *Listing how their feelings change with different situations and experiences.*
    c. *Monitoring physical feelings and emotions when actually encountering these situations.*
    d. *Correctly identifying and labeling these feelings.*
    e. *Communicating these feelings so others can understand them.*

5. Explain to students it is important as they rotate through the stations that they respond to others' feelings in an appropriate way so that all students feel comfortable sharing. Remind students to use the Boys Town Social Skill **Responding to the Feelings of Others** during this activity by:
    a. *Listening to the other person.*
    b. *Acknowledging what they are saying or writing.*
    c. *Expressing concern or empathy when appropriate.*
    d. *Offering to help or provide advice if the other person wants it.*
    e. *Encouraging the person to seek additional help, if necessary.*

6. Instruct students to begin with an assigned station. Provide about 5 minutes.

7. Instruct students to switch stations. Continue until all students have been at each station.

8. When students have had enough time to respond to each category, review the suggestions and lists made at each station. Ask the students for feedback to what has been written and shared.

9. Instruct each student to write down one thing they learned about themselves and being "rescued" from schoolwork or something at school. Ask them to show it to you as they leave the class.

FLIPPED CLASSROOM:

This lesson could be placed on a class blog or website. Students respond to the questions in each category by recording their answers on a piece of paper. Begin class by covering the social skills in the lesson and then ask students to share their responses with the class. Conclude the class time with step six of the Teacher Instructions.

Recognizing the Signs

OBJECTIVES:

Social Skills: Students will practice accepting help or assistance and declining help or assistance.

Executive Functions: Students will understand they will need to exhibit more grit instead of accepting too much help. They will also show gratitude by graciously accepting help when needed.

MATERIALS NEEDED:

- Paper
- Pencil
- Chart Paper
- "You Said, They Should Have Said" T-chart worksheet
- Boys Town Social Skill poster, "Accepting Help or Assistance"

 There are times in life when we must take a life preserver or let someone rescue us, but there are also times when we can work it out on our own or with minimal help.

TEACHER INSTRUCTIONS:

1. **Prior to class,** select and bookmark an online video of the lifecycle of a butterfly.

2. During class ask students to recall what they know about butterflies and specifically about the lifecycle of a butterfly. Emphasize the concept of metamorphosis.

3. Give students two to three minutes to recall and discuss with a partner what would happen if this process were interrupted, and to record any ideas of what would happen to the butterfly if someone tried to help this process along. (Refer to Lesson 1 "Defining Rescue".)

4. Show the video you have selected.

5. Explain to the students that the struggle the butterfly goes through to get out of the chrysalis is actually what is necessary to enable it to fly. The head, abdomen, and legs come out first, but because the wings don't work yet they have to stay there for a while longer until the fluid has been pumped through the abdomen and then dries. It has to go through this effort and waiting so that it is prepared and capable of flying. If we help the butterfly along and try to speed up this process it would make it very difficult, if not impossible, for the butterfly to ever be able to fly.

6. Ask the students how someone helping them too much could actually be hurting them. Record on the board or chart paper.

7. Give each pair of students a "You Said, They Should Have Said" T-chart worksheet. Explain that just as people don't mean to hurt the butterfly by trying to help it out of its struggle, people offer to help us so we don't have to struggle. On the "You Said" side of the chart, list things you say to try to get people to "rescue" you. On the "They Should Have Said" side, record what they should say to someone without "rescuing" him or her. *(For example, "You Said" "This is impossible!" "They Said" "Here, let me help you get started.")*

8. Remember, it is okay to occasionally accept a little help when you are struggling, or there may be times when you choose to decline someone's assistance. The Boys Town Social Skill **Accepting Help or Assistance** includes steps:
   a. *Look at the person offering help.*
   b. *Sincerely thank him or her for helping.*
   c. *If help is not needed, politely decline the person's assistance.*
   d. *If help is needed, accept the help or advice and again thank the person.*

9. Practice role-playing the examples that the students list on the T-chart by using this social skill.

FLIPPED CLASSROOM:
Ask students to watch an online video of the lifecycle of a butterfly before coming to class.

NAME:_____

DATE:_____

ACTIVITY

You Said, They Should Have Said

DIRECTIONS: The chart below has two columns. Under the "YOU SAID" column, list things you have said (or heard someone say) when trying to be rescued. Under the "THEY SHOULD HAVE SAID" column, write an alternative response that would show support but allow someone to work through a problem instead of being rescued.

YOU SAID	THEY SHOULD HAVE SAID
This is impossible!	Here, let me help you get started and then you can take it from there.
I'm never going to get this!	Focus on the 1st step to begin.
I don't understand.	What part don't you understand? **OR**
	Tell me what you do understand and we'll go from there.
Can you do it for me?	I can't do it for you, but I would be happy to help you.
This will never work.	It might take a little effort but I think you can get it to work. Can I help you get started?
I think I can do this.	Yes, you can!

Attitude Adjustment, Seeing Problems as Opportunities

OBJECTIVES:

Social Skills: Students will identify the steps needed for effective problem-solving. Students will understand they can choose to see problems as opportunities.

Executive Functions: Students will display curiosity and zest by exploring possible solutions with enthusiasm.

MATERIALS NEEDED:

- Paper
- Pencil
- Dictionaries
- Wide assortment of problem-solving games and puzzles (see step 1)
- Boys Town Social Skill poster, "Using Structured Problem Solving (SODAS)"

TEACHER INSTRUCTIONS:

1. Scatter several brain boosting, problem-solving games around the room. These could include crossword puzzles, Sudoku, chess, checkers, mystery puzzles, 3-D puzzles, computer brain activities, etc.

2. Give the students time to explore the games and puzzles to warm up their problem-solving thinking before going on to the next step.

3. Give the students 90 seconds to write down their definition of what a problem is. Merriam Webster defines a problem as "something that is difficult to deal with: something that is a source of trouble, worry, etc."

4. Give the students 90 seconds to write down their definition of what an opportunity is. Merriam Webster defines an opportunity as "a good chance for advancement or progress."

5. Ask the students to write down the following statement in their assignment book or somewhere where they will see it daily. "I will see problems as opportunities!" Instruct students to write down what they think this statement means and how it relates to the definitions above. Share ideas.

6. Pose the following problem to the students:
"It has come to the staff's attention that someone has been opening and rummaging through other students' lockers without their permission. This must be stopped. It is your job today to select a partner and invent a way to catch whoever is doing this. You will need to make a sample of your idea. Do not tell anyone how it works or what it specifically is because you do not want to tip off the locker intruder."

7. Explain to students they should use the following steps of the Boys Town Social Skill **Using Structured Problem Solving (SODAS)**:
   a. *Define the problem or "**S**"ituation.*
   b. *Generate two or more "**O**"ptions.*
   c. *Look at each option's potential "**D**"isadvantages.*
   d. *Look at each option's potential "**A**"dvantages.*
   e. *Decide on the best "**S**"olution.*

Emphasize how they can remember these steps by remembering SODAS.

8. Explain to students that all the ideas will be unveiled the following class period, and provide them time to work.

9. **The following class period** begins by asking students to summarize the problem from the previous period. Through this activity, how could they see the problem as an opportunity? Discuss until the students see the correlation between problems and opportunities. (One of the opportunities could be this type of invention could make everyone's lockers more secure. Another opportunity could be trying to solve this problem can promote teamwork. Thirdly, the opportunity is they can catch the person.)

10. Request the students share their ideas of how to catch the locker intruder.

11. After the presentations, vote for the best idea.

12. Ask the students to explain what would have happened if they would have chosen to only see the problem and not the opportunity. *(Answer: they would still have the problem and wouldn't have any ideas of how to stop it or catch the intruder; therefore missing the opportunity.)*

Use a wide assortment of puzzles including ones from online sources. Brainteasers are another option.

FLIPPED CLASSROOM:

Prior to coming to class, ask students to find a definition of the following words: "problem" and "opportunity" and how they can practice turning problems into opportunities. Ask them to have a solution for the locker intruder scenario before coming to class. Use the time in class to explore the solutions further and vote on the best idea.

ADDITIONAL RESOURCES:

Online brainteasers or puzzle challenges.

Mountains of Problems or Not?

OBJECTIVES:

Social Skills: Students will practice setting goals in order to turn their problem into an opportunity.

Executive Functions: Students will display optimism in seeing the opportunities in their problems.

MATERIALS NEEDED:

- Paper
- Pencil
- Construction paper for problem rocks
- Tissue paper or another more transparent paper for the opportunity rock
- Markers
- "Paper Rock Template" handout
- Boys Town Social Skill poster, "Setting Goals"

 Often, students only see the problems in their life and not the opportunities for growth and development. We need to encourage them to look for the opportunities even if it requires work on their part.

TEACHER INSTRUCTIONS:

1. Review the definition of a problem from the previous lesson. (Merriam Webster defines a problem as "something that is difficult to deal with: something that is a source of trouble, worry, etc.")

2. Review the definition of an opportunity from the previous lesson. (Merriam Webster defines an opportunity as "a good chance for advancement or progress.")

3. Explain to the students problems can build on each other until you arrive at a mountain that is very hard to overcome. Students can share examples of this from their own lives.

4. Give students a "Paper Rock Template" and have them write down one problem they face on the rock. Construct a mountain on the wall by taping the rock shapes on top of each other.

5. Provide students with another rock shape made out of tissue paper or another more transparent type of paper. Ask students to write down one opportunity that can come out of the problem they wrote on the first rock shape. Be careful not to rip the tissue paper while writing the opportunity. (Using the tissue paper allows the students to view the problem behind the opportunity.) Tape or staple the tissue paper opportunity rock over the problem rock on the mountain of problems.

6. Instruct the students to write the following quote in a place where they will see it regularly: "Problems are only opportunities in work clothes," by Henri Kaiser.

7. Allow time for discussion as to what this quote means. Explain to the students there is now a mountain of opportunities instead of a mountain of problems. Eventually express to the students we can turn our problems into opportunities but we don't always recognize this because it can take a lot of work.

8. To help a person succeed in turning a problem into an opportunity it is important to know how to set goals. Present the Boys Town Social Skill **Setting Goals** to the students:
   a. *Decide on your overall values and lifestyle desires.*
   b. *List the resources you need to fulfill these lifestyle options.*
   c. *Examine the intermediate steps in accomplishing your overall outcome.*
   d. *Establish short- and long-term goals that will help you accomplish the steps necessary for the desired outcome.*

9. Using the guidelines in step 8, ask the students to write down the steps they would take into turning their problem into the opportunity they recorded.

Goal-setting is a hard task for some students. Some will need guidance in setting specific and deliberate steps towards reaching their desired goal.

Paper Rock Template

My problem is
that I don't have anyone
at home that can help
me with my homework.

NOTE: On the second rock (opportunity) they would write: I could find new friends to call or it could make me get better at my time management while I'm at school.

SECTION 2

The "Stinkin' Thinkin'!"

When a person dwells on a negative problem or situation it becomes damaging and can prevent the ability to move on. We beat ourselves up with guilt and a "wish things were different" type of thinking. Negative thinking is always focusing on what is wrong with life, whereas positive thinking helps us to see what is right with our lives and the world. Students need to understand and recognize harmful, negative ways of thinking and realize these are bad habits that need to be corrected. To get rid of negativity, one has to be aware of the thought processes that occur. It helps to pay closer attention to our automatic thoughts.

As educators, one of our jobs is to help students get rid of toxic ways of thinking. This will allow us to start retraining the thinking process and reduce the amount of negative self-talk that occurs in our students.

Students may not be able to get rid of all negative thinking, but through reflection they can adopt steps to help them learn and change.

Activities included in this section are:
- **Take Out the Trash!**
- **Where Does It Start?**
- **Bad Habits Are Hard to Break**
- **Negative News**
- **Are You Stuck?**

Take Out the Trash!

OBJECTIVES:

Social Skills: Students will identify ways to stop a negative or harmful thought.

Executive Functions: Students will realize self-control allows them to be able to stop negative thoughts and replace them with positive thoughts.

MATERIALS NEEDED:

- Pencil or other writing utensil
- Scissors
- Tape
- Smelly trash in a trash can
- "Cube Template" handout
- Boys Town Social Skill poster, "Stopping Negative or Harmful Thoughts"

 Students can get into a "rut" with negative or "stinkin' thinkin'." In order to be more successful it is important to identify the negative thoughts and start replacing them with more positive messages.

TEACHER INSTRUCTIONS:

1. **Prior to class,** obtain a trash can with smelly trash in it. You will want the students to notice the smell as they enter the room.

2. **During class,** as students start commenting on the bad smell start walking around holding the trash can closer to the desks or tables in the room. Tell students this smelly trash represents "stinkin' thinkin'" that you sometimes see from some of them.

3. Generate a list with the students on what they think "stinkin' thinkin'" is. Emphasize this type of thinking or behavior results in:
    a. students not trying hard on assignments or activities;
    b. students criticizing and getting down on themselves;
    c. perhaps they have a helpless mentality by thinking they will never understand the lesson they are struggling with; or,
    d. they might have the viewpoint nothing good ever happens to them, or that nobody likes them.

    Record as many of these types of ideas or statements as possible.

4. Refer back to the trash at this point and ask the students how you could get rid of the smell or the "stink." Make sure to relate their suggestions back to "stinkin' thinkin'." Below are a few suggestions of how to explain some answers you might receive:
    a. Bury the really smelly object deeper into the trashcan.
       (Burying the trash deeper will not really get rid of the entire smell because it is still in there. This is like trying to bury our hurt feelings or feelings of failure. They might not be as noticeable at first but they will eventually surface again.)
    b. Spray the trashcan with air fresheners.
       (This might cover up the smell, but the fresheners will eventually be overtaken by the smell again. We can act like we are thinking positive on the outside, but unless we change how we feel and think, it is just a cover-up.)
    c. The only way to really get rid of the smell is to take out the trash and replace the dirty trash bag with a fresh, new one.
       (The only way to get rid of our negative thinking is to get it out of our minds and replace it with positive thoughts.)

5. Explain to students they CAN stop negative or harmful thoughts. The best way to do this is to follow the steps in the Boys Town Social Skill **Stopping Negative or Harmful Thoughts**:
    a. *Identify negative or repetitive thoughts you wish to avoid.*
    b. *When these occur, consistently say to yourself "Stop!"*
    c. *Immediately visualize a more positive scene/statement or relaxing thought.*
    d. *Reward yourself for using strategies to stop your negative or harmful thoughts.*

    Discuss each step with the students.

6. Distribute a "Cube Template" to each student.

7. Instruct students to write a positive statement or one of the steps listed above from the Boys Town Social Skill on each of the six sides.

8. Have students cut out the cubes and tape together. These can be kept at their desk so they can look at them if they are struggling with "stinkin' thinkin'." Possible statements could include:

    a. I'll do better next time.

    b. I'm doing better.

    c. I will get this!

    d. I can always improve.

    e. I am learning.

    f. Mistakes help me improve.

    g. I am not helpless.

Generate a list of positive statements of your own as a resource for students who are struggling.

Cube Template

I'll do
better next
time.

Identify negative
or repetitive
thoughts you
wish to avoid.

I will
get this!

I am
learning!

Mistakes
help me
improve.

When negative
thoughts occur
I will say to
myself, "Stop!"

DIRECTIONS: Write a positive statement or one of the Boys Town Social Skills steps to "Stopping Negative or Harmful Thoughts" on each of the six sides. Cut out the cube and tape together.

Where Does It Start?

OBJECTIVES:

Social Skills: Students will practice reducing or eliminating negative or harmful thoughts.

Executive Functions: Students will practice self-control by reducing or eliminating negative thoughts.

MATERIALS NEEDED:

- Supply of 8 ½" x 11" paper, cut into fourths
- Pencil
- Set of problem flashcards
- Supply of 9" x 12" paper, cut in half (9" x 6")
- Boys Town Social Skill poster, "Stopping Negative or Harmful Thoughts"

TEACHER INSTRUCTIONS:

1. **Prior to class,** make a set of flashcards that contain areas where negative thoughts or problems can originate. See list of suggestions under Additional Resources. Start with 8-10 possible problems.

2. **During class,** review the Take Out the Trash! lesson. Ask students to summarize what this lesson was about. (*Possible answer: You have to get rid of negative thoughts and replace them with positive thoughts.*)

3. To make this task easier, it is important to know where some of those negative thoughts originate. Give each student 8-10 pieces of paper. (This is the 8 ½" x 11" paper cut into fourths.)

4. Ask students to number the pages. As you show the students each flash card, ask them to write down either a "P" for problem or an "O" for opportunity on the piece of paper numbered to match the order of your flashcards. (Instruct students to be sure to use a different piece of paper for each one.)

5. Display the flashcards in order after showing them so the students can refer to them later.

6. After sharing all the flashcards, ask the students to go back and write down any negative thoughts they have concerning the area each card represents. (Have students focus on the "P" or problem cards since if they see it as an "O" (opportunity) they have already started down the path of positive thinking for that topic.)

7. Once the students have written down their negative thoughts on all of the pieces of paper, instruct them to wad up that piece of paper and throw it away. Explain they need to get rid of negative thoughts surrounding the obstacle.

8. Review the following steps with the students of the Boys Town Social Skill **Stopping Negative or Harmful Thoughts:**
   a. *Identify negative or repetitive thoughts you wish to avoid.*
   b. *When these occur, consistently say to yourself "Stop!"*
   c. *Immediately visualize a more positive scene/statement or relaxing thought.*
   d. *Reward yourself for using strategies to stop your negative or harmful thoughts.*

9. Ask students to get a new piece of paper for each one they threw away and write down how they can now see these challenges or problems as opportunities. Remind students it is necessary to retrain our brain to eliminate negative thinking. *(Example: If they picked "peer pressure" as a problem, then an opportunity might be to practice being more independent.)*

10. Give each student a piece of plain white paper measuring 9" x 6" and have them do the following:
    a. Fold the paper in half like a hotdog (will be 9" x 3").
    b. Place the paper fold at the bottom like an upside down table tent.

11. Instruct students to write the word "problem" on one side of the paper in cursive handwriting. Each letter needs to touch the fold line.

12. Turn the paper over and hold up to a window. Trace the word on the other side of the paper. It will appear to be upside down, but the lines of the letter should touch. (See example on page 31.)

13. Open up the paper and ask students to create something out of the words. It could be a design, creature, geometric design, etc.

14. Display in the classroom to help students remember to look at their problems as opportunities.

FLIPPED CLASSROOM:

Ask students to look online and generate a list of eight areas that could be the source of negative thinking or problems. Place each problem area on a separate, small piece of paper. Record any negative thought about each of the eight areas. *(Example: Testing, "I freeze during tests and never know anything.")* Ask students to bring the ideas to class. Begin class the following day with step 4 of the Teacher Instructions.

ADDITIONAL RESOURCES:

List of possible problems or negative thoughts for flash cards:

Peer pressure

Being stressed out

Overextended (too many activities)

Testing

Puberty or changes in the body

Don't understand their feelings

Social drama

Peer acceptance

Organizational skills

Hard work

New school

Don't feel connected to others

Family problems

Want attention

Mad at someone

Mad at self

It's raining

Don't feel well

Get an award

Challenging work

Making the "A" team

Etc.

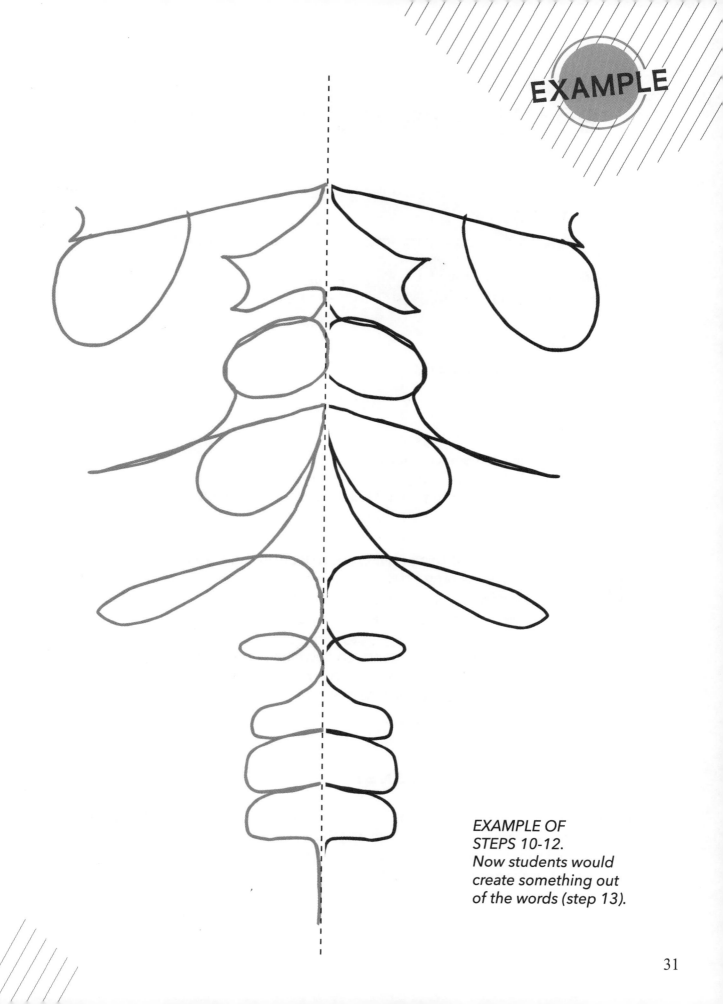

*EXAMPLE OF
STEPS 10-12.
Now students would
create something out
of the words (step 13).*

31

Bad Habits Are Hard To Break

OBJECTIVES:

Social Skills: Students will practice showing sensitivity to others.

Executive Functions: Students will display social intelligence by demonstrating respect for the feelings of others.

MATERIALS NEEDED:

- Paper
- Pencil
- Tissues
- iPads, tablets, other electronic devices
- Downloaded Type Drawing Apps (see below)
- Boys Town Social Skill poster, "Showing Sensitivity to Others"

The goals of this activity are to identify bad or negative habits, such as NEGATIVE THINKING, and to recognize it is easier to break a bad habit right when it starts, rather than waiting until after you have been doing it for a longer period of time.

Step 5 requires students to download an app. If your school policy requires permission in advance, or in the interest of time, you may want to handle this prior to the day of the lesson.

TEACHER INSTRUCTIONS:

1. **One day prior to this lesson,** remind students to bring any iPads, tablets, phones or other electronic devices to class for this activity. (You may want to communicate with parents via email to let them know about the activity to increase the likelihood parents will allow the devices to come to school with the student.)

2. Ask the students how hard it would be to tear one tissue in half. *(Easy.)* Tear the tissue in half.

3. Show a stack of tissues to the students and ask how easy it would be to tear them in half. *(More difficult.)* Ask for a volunteer to try to tear them in half. Make sure to have several so that the task becomes difficult for the student.

4. Instruct students to select a partner and generate ideas of how this could be similar to breaking bad habits. Discuss all ideas. During the discussion, emphasize how tearing the tissues symbolizes how it is easier to break a bad habit in the beginning rather than after you have been doing it for a longer period of time. It is also easier to break a bad or negative habit when it is just your habit and not a habit of a whole group.

5. With the iPads, tablets and other devices, download any free Type Drawing App. Patext, TextsPhoto, and Rage Comic Maker are a few choices.

6. Inform students they will be taking or drawing pictures of bad habits, and they need to be sensitive to others when taking those pictures. Review the steps of the Boys Town Social Skill **Showing Sensitivity to Others** with the class:
   a. *Express interest and concern for others, especially when they are having trouble or have a bad habit.*
   b. *Recognize that disabled people deserve the same respect as anyone else.*
   c. *Apologize or make amends for hurting someone's feelings or causing harm.*
   d. *Recognize that people of different races, religions, and backgrounds deserve to be treated the same way as you would expect to be treated.*

7. Explain to students that what that means for this activity is:
   a. Students must ask permission before taking someone's picture.
   b. Students must respect the answer (no or yes).
   c. Only school-appropriate pictures are allowed.
   d. Once the picture is taken, students should thank the person.
   e. Students must be respectful with the picture (i.e., no posting on social media, forwarding, or doing anything other than using it for this assignment).
   f. The original picture should be deleted when the assignment is complete.

8. Ask each pair of students to take photos or download pictures of bad habits they see occurring, or to draw with the tools on the app any bad habit they feel people could have.

9. Add text to the photo or picture to identify the bad habit and how to break it.

10. Share photos and pictures with the class and to your class blog or website. Post ways the bad or negative habit could be broken.

Make sure students have permission to download free apps. Review the importance of only taking school appropriate photos and to be sensitive of the people's feelings in the photo. Arrange for extra electronic devices.

FLIPPED CLASSROOM:

Prior to class, ask students to take a photo or find a picture of a bad habit. Use the photo editor to add text to the photo stating why it is a bad habit and how to break it. Print the picture or save and email to the teacher. View the photos in class and discuss.

 Emphasize taking appropriate pictures before giving the assignment.

ADDITIONAL RESOURCES:

Free online photo editing sites. Access to electronic devices.

Negative News

OBJECTIVES:

Social Skills: Students will choose appropriate words to use when rewriting newspaper articles.

Executive Functions: Students will show grit by working independently with focus. They will also show social intelligence by respecting others' feelings with the words they choose to write.

MATERIALS NEEDED:

- Paper
- Small slips of paper
- Pencil
- Transparent glass, half-filled with water
- Newspaper articles (paper or online)
- Dictionaries, thesauruses
- Small cup for slips of paper
- Boys Town Social Skill poster, "Choosing Appropriate Words"

TEACHER INSTRUCTIONS:

1. **Prior to class,** set a glass on the table. Fill the glass half-way with water.

2. **During class,** once the students are seated, ask them to describe what they see in writing. Share descriptions.

3. Poll students to see how many saw the glass as half-empty and how many saw the glass as half-full. Explain that, while this was a simple activity and doesn't necessarily represent a person's thought processes in every situation, those who saw the glass as half-full are generally considered to be more optimistic than those who saw it as half-empty.

4. Explain to students the mind is fairly neutral; however what we say to ourselves over and over cultivates and determines whether we see life through a positive or negative lens.

5. Project two or three newspaper articles from your computer.

6. Read the articles as a class and analyze whether they were written from a negative or positive viewpoint. (Many newspaper articles report on negative stories.) Ask students to speculate on what this means for how we see the world. *(Answer: We will think there is more negative happenings in the world.)*

7. Place an empty cup in the front of the room on a flat table or desk.

8. Instruct students to answer the following question on a small piece of paper, and place their answer to the question in the cup at the front of the room when they are finished: "Why don't we find more positive articles in the newspaper?"

9. Once everyone has added their answers to the cup, read all of the answers out loud, and discuss with the class how this affects the way we view the world.

10. Provide students time to select a newspaper article (online or hard copy). Explain the purpose of the article – they will rewrite the article from a positive perspective.

11. Remind students of the importance of **Choosing Appropriate Words** when rewriting the articles. It is important to:
   a. *Look at the situation and the people around you.*
      (Example: How could you best rewrite the article so they understand it?)
   b. *Know the meanings of words you are about to say/write.*
   c. *Refrain from using words that will offend people around you or that they will not understand.*
   d. *Avoid using slang, profanity, or words that could have a sexual meaning.*
   e. *Decide what thought you want to put into words and then say/write the words.*

12. Provide dictionaries and thesauruses for the students to use.

13. Give the students time to complete their rewrite of the article (or assign as homework).

14. When the articles are turned in, share a few with the class.

 Have newspaper articles available for students who might not have Internet access.

FLIPPED CLASSROOM:

Ask students to choose an online newspaper(s) of their choice. Select two or three stories and critique whether they are written from a positive or a negative viewpoint. Write a paragraph explaining the viewpoint chosen for each article. Bring to class. Share in class and then proceed with step 7 under the Teacher Instructions.

ADDITIONAL RESOURCES:

Online news sources.

Are You Stuck?

OBJECTIVES:

Social Skills: Students will learn the importance of analyzing tasks to be completed.

Executive Functions: Students will exhibit grit by trying hard after experiencing failure, and display optimism by getting over frustrations and setbacks quickly.

MATERIALS NEEDED:

- Paper
- Pencil
- Popsicle sticks (mini or regular)
- Cup or container
- Fine tip markers in various colors
- "Paper Brick Template" handout
- (Optional) Wood blocks (instead of Paper Bricks Template)
- Boys Town Social Skill poster, "Analyzing Tasks to Be Completed"

TEACHER INSTRUCTIONS:

1. **Prior to class,** gather all materials in a central location and determine how you will have students proceed with the activity given the layout of the room,

2. **During class,** tell students that you will be constructing a brick wall out of paper (the paper bricks) or wood blocks.

3. **If using the paper bricks:**
   a. Pass out the "Paper Bricks Template" to each student.
   b. Have students cut out and assemble the paper brick.

4. If using wood blocks inform students of the procedure for picking up a block.

5. Ask each student to place a block on the wall. Refer to the wall as the Negative Thinking Wall.

6. Ask students what is meant when people say that they have "hit a brick wall." *(Answer: They feel like they can't go any further or they don't have any more ideas. They feel stuck.)* Have students share when they have felt like this at school.

7. On a piece of paper, instruct students to write down five ways they could get past the brick wall built by the class, or any brick wall. *(Climb it, hammer it down, smash it, go around it, build a bridge over it, etc.)*

8. Ask students to think of ways they could get through the brick wall that they sometimes hit at school because of their negative thinking. Have students list five of them on a piece of paper.

9. Tell each student to select their top two suggestions and verbally share them with the class. *(Examples: Get a clue from a buddy or take a quick break and look at it again, tell yourself you can get it, etc.)*

10. Explain to students that sometimes they "hit a brick wall" because they have not properly analyzed the tasks that needed to be completed. Take some time to review the Boys Town Social Skill **Analyzing Tasks to Be Completed** with the class:
   a. *Clarify what task or assignment has been given to you.*
   b. *List every step that you need to do in order to complete the task.*
   c. *Identify which step needs to be done first, second, third, etc.*
   d. *Begin completing the steps in order.*

11. Give each student two Popsicle sticks and a fine tip marker.

12. Ask students to write each suggestion from Teacher Instruction step 9 on a Popsicle stick. Place the completed Popsicle sticks in a cup or container in a designated spot in the room.

13. Identify a student in the class to add the steps of the Boys Town Social Skill **Analyzing Tasks to Be Completed** (one step per Popsicle stick).

14. Explain to students the suggestions on the Popsicle sticks will be for all students to use. When they get stuck on a problem or activity or if they feel like they have hit a brick wall, students can select a Popsicle stick out of the cup to help them gain a different viewpoint and get the encouragement needed to keep going or try something different.

Paper Brick Template

DIRECTIONS: Cut out the brick and tape together.
Place the block on the Negative Thinking Wall.

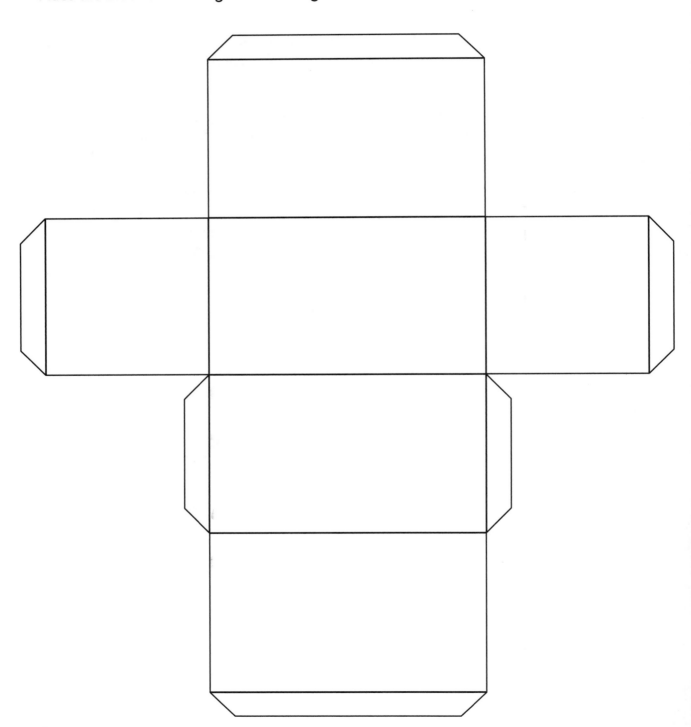

SECTION 3

Let's Get Positive

Students sabotage their chances of academic success by allowing toxic, negative thinking to take place. Finding ways to control the "weeds" in our mind can clear the way for healthier ways of thinking, which can lead to success. We must also guard the words we use. Words have a huge impact on our emotions so we must equally work on replacing negative words with positive ones. Learning alternative strategies to overcome negative thinking is a good step in cultivating a more positive behavior and outlook.

Taking time to explore our creativity not only promotes positive thinking but it can also give us new and varied perspectives to problems we are facing. Creativity can build confidence within an individual by emphasizing one's uniqueness. Furthermore, laughter can trigger positive thinking by giving us an optimistic outlook on life's problems, stresses, and difficult situations. Laughter is contagious so therefore we can spread positive thinking.

Activities included in this section are:

- Get Rid of the Toxins
- Pushing the "Pepper" Out!
- Vocab Makeover!
- Get Creative!
- LOL!

Get Rid of the Toxins

OBJECTIVES:

Social Skills: Students will distinguish appropriate ways to ask for help when needed.

Executive Functions: Students will show optimism by realizing that reducing negative thinking and "toxic weeds" will improve their future.

MATERIALS NEEDED:

- Paper
- Pencil
- Various varieties of weeds
- Bag for the weeds
- "Toxic Weeds/Healthy Plant" worksheet
- Boys Town Social Skill poster, "Asking For Help"

 What do students do that can decrease their chances of academic success? Negative thinking is one way students harm themselves. Our job is to help them get rid of the toxins or toxic ways of thinking and replace them with healthier habits to clear the way for success. Even if we can't eliminate all the "weeds," we can control them so they don't intrude on our healthy lifestyle habits and thinking.

TEACHER INSTRUCTIONS

1. **Prior to class,** collect various weeds from the yard or garden. Place in a bag.

2. **During class,** pull the weeds out of the bag and ask the students what they are. Ask them to tell you what they know about weeds and why most people don't like weeds. *(Answer: They quickly*

kill the good plants or grass.) Ask students what happens if we don't get rid of the weeds in the grass or garden? Do they change the way the yard or garden looks?

3. Explain that the examples you are showing in class are the kinds of weeds we can see. Suggest that there are "weeds" we can't see in our own life. Brainstorm what this might mean.

4. Explain the "weeds" are the toxins in our life. These toxins are like the negative thinking that has been discussed in previous lessons. Ask students to brainstorm different toxins they encounter at school. Generate a list on the board or on a piece of chart paper. *(Bullying, gossip, laziness, etc.)*

5. Distribute the "Toxic Weeds/Healthy Plant" worksheet. Instruct students to write a toxin on next to each weed that represents something they need to get rid of in order to be more successful. *(Examples: lack of confidence, working too rapidly, not listening to instructions, being mean to someone, excluding someone, yelling, lack of grit, giving up, toxic friends, gossip, etc.)*

6. Ask students the following questions:
   a. Have the weeds in your life changed the way you act and think?
   b. Do people see you as a toxic weed? If so, can you change that?
   c. What will you do to get the "weeds" out of your mind and life?
   d. Is it difficult to get rid of all the weeds? Why or why not?
   e. Is it okay to ask for help with this task? How could you ask for help?

7. Explain to students asking for help is a great skill, though tough for many. The important thing about knowing when to ask for help is to make sure you give it your all and are willing to keep going. Teach the following steps of the Boys Town Social Skill **Asking for Help**:
   a. *Look at the person*
   b. *Ask the person if he or she has time to help you (now or later).*
   c. *Clearly describe the problem or what kind of help you need.*
   d. *Thank the person for helping you.*

8. Return to asking students the following questions, and discussing:
   a. Can getting rid of the negative, toxic weeds turn you back into the healthy, beautiful person you are to be? *(Yes.)*
   b. Will it be possible to always get rid of all the "weeds?" *(Answer: Probably not, but we can keep them under control so they don't take over our healthy lifestyle habits.)*

9. Express to students getting rid of the toxic weeds is important but it is also important to replace them with something better or positive. Explain they will practice turning a toxin into something better or something non-toxic. This toxin will have the potential to become a healthy plant.

10. Refer back to the "Toxic Weeds/Healthy Plant" worksheet. Instruct students that next to each weed on the worksheet there is a healthy plant. Have them write one thing they will do to replace the corresponding toxic weed with a healthier, more productive behavior.

There is a better selection of outdoor weeds in the spring, summer, and fall.

NAME:_____

DATE:_____

Toxic Weeds/Healthy Plant

DIRECTIONS: Write an example of a "TOXIN" beside each picture of a weed. The toxin represents something you need to get rid of in order to be more successful. (Example: working too fast, lack of grit, etc.) Next to "HEALTHY PLANT," write one way you could replace the toxic weed with something healthier to be more successful.

TOXIC WEED: Putting my homework off until the last minute / procrastination

HEALTHY PLANT: Set a time to study right after school before I do other things.

TOXIC WEED: Skimming the text for answers instead of reading thoroughly

HEALTHY PLANT: Slow down and read all of the material before working on questions.

TOXIC WEED: Gossip

HEALTHY PLANT: Don't say anything to anyone or about anyone, unless it is nice.

TOXIC WEED: Giving up easily

HEALTHY PLANT: Stick with it Show GRIT by working hard.

Pushing the "Pepper" Out!

OBJECTIVES:

Social Skills: Students will demonstrate their abilities to take alternative steps (alter their environments) to overcome negative thinking and habits.

Executive Functions: Students will demonstrate grit by trying hard even if they are experiencing failure.

MATERIALS NEEDED:

- Paper
- Pencil
- Bowl of water
- Pepper
- Dish soap
- Video from the Internet of someone overcoming an obstacle (see step 7)
- "Pushing The Pepper Out Again Twitter Board" (a long piece of butcher paper displayed somewhere in the room that allows you to post and erase different messages throughout the year; choose a width that can go through the laminator.)
- Markers (non-permanent) for writing on the "Pushing the Pepper Out Again Twitter Board"
- Boys Town Social Skill poster, "Altering One's Environment"

 Students may struggle and fail with eliminating their negative thinking or "toxic weeds" all of the time. They will need to be encouraged to get back up and try again. Eventually, they will have more positive thinking than negative thinking.

TEACHER INSTRUCTIONS:

1. **Prior to class,** hang the "Pushing the Pepper Out Again Twitter Board."

2. **During class,** ask students how they are doing with replacing their negative thoughts with positive ones. Ask for input on whether it is easy or difficult and why they feel this way.

3. Put a small bowl of water on a table. The bowl will represent their brain.

4. Select a student to sprinkle a good amount of pepper in the bowl. The pepper will represent negative thinking or "toxic weeds" from the previous lesson.

5. Select another student to pour some dish soap into the bowl. The dish soap represents positive thinking or healthier habits. Observe the outcome.

6. Ask for suggestions on how this is like replacing negative thoughts with positive ones. *(Answer: When we first put in positive thoughts or habits, the negative moves to the side but then starts to float back in. We have to keep putting in the positive to keep the negative out of the way.)* Remind students they will not always succeed at this. It takes practice and retraining the brain.

7. Show a video clip of someone overcoming an obstacle. The Internet has many sources of videos of individuals who have overcome great odds to succeed by not quitting. Select one you feel your students would relate well to. (One example is the video clip of Derek Redmond running the 400-meter sprint in the 1992 Barcelona Olympics.)

8. Ask students to reflect on how difficult it would have been to overcome the obstacle. Encourage them to share their thoughts and opinions. Relate this to how hard it can be to overcome negative thoughts and bad habits.

9. Instruct students to write down one way they will get back up and "push the pepper" out again when they think negatively or give in to their bad habit. Ask them to also share this information as a written "tweet" on the class "Pushing the Pepper Out Again Twitter Board."

10. Introduce the "Pushing the Pepper Out Again Twitter Board" (the butcher paper you have laminated and displayed) and explain it works like a Twitter feed. As part of their grade, you could require students to tweet something once a week about how they are continuing to work on pushing negative thoughts and bad habits out and putting positive thoughts into their minds, using twitter language and symbols.

11. Have each student write down and hand in an identifying name so you can track their comments each week without other students knowing who wrote a comment. (Or use whatever

method makes it easiest for you to monitor the comments.) The board serves as a constant visual reminder of how students are trying to overcome negative thinking.

12. Explain to students this activity will require them to use the Boys Town Social Skill **Altering One's Environment**:

    a. *Identify situations in which you encounter difficulty.*

    b. *Look for parts of those situations that could be changed to bring about improvement.*

    c. *Make appropriate changes to improve self-esteem, behavior, or performance.*

. . . .

 Use enough pepper to get the full effect.

. . . .

FLIPPED CLASSROOM:

Post video links, either online or on the class website/blog, about individuals who kept "Pushing the Pepper Out" when they had negative thoughts. Ask students to watch the videos and write down three ways they overcame their negative thinking or bad habit. Have students share their lists in class and then continue with the lesson.

ADDITIONAL RESOURCES:

Examples of "tweets" or instructions for using Twitter.

Vocab Makeover!

OBJECTIVES:

Social Skills: Students will practice working independently.

Executive Functions: Students will show grit by working independently with focus.

MATERIALS NEEDED:

- Paper
- Pencil
- Chart paper
- Markers
- "Vocab Makeover" worksheet
- Boys Town Social Skill poster, "Working Independently"
- (Optional) Access to computers

 Just like our thoughts have a huge impact on our behavior, our words have a huge impact on our emotions. We must work to erase words that exemplify "negative thinking" from our vocabulary.

TEACHER INSTRUCTIONS:

1. **Prior to class,** hang two pieces of chart paper in the classroom, with a variety of markers.

2. **During class,** instruct students to generate two lists of words. On one sheet of paper write down all the negative meaning words that come to mind, such as "can't," "should," "might not," "never," etc. On the second sheet of paper write down all the positive meaning words that come to mind such as "can," "will," "today," etc.

3. Compare the two lists. Decide which list was easier to make and why. (The negative one will probably be easier.)

4. Give each student a copy of the "Vocab Makeover" worksheet and provide the following instructions:

    a. On the negative words side, ask students to select six negative words from the class list (or think of six of their own) and place them in the "Cause" boxes.

    b. In the two "Effect" boxes for each "Cause" list two effects that using the negative word could possibly have on a person. (See worksheet example.)

    c. On the other side of the worksheet, complete using six positive words and the effect they could have on a person. (See worksheet example.)

    d. Explain to the class that thinking of "effects" may be difficult for some students, but it is important to work independently in order to better process the information.

5. Review the steps of the Boys Town Social Skill **Working Independently** with the students:

    a. Start on tasks promptly without procrastinating.

    b. Remain on-task without being reminded.

    c. Continue working unprompted until the task is completed.

    d. Check back with the person who assigned the task.

6. **For several days after this lesson,** try to reward those students who practice using positive words instead of negative. Examples might be free time, verbal praise, a "good job" slip of paper, or another reward of your choice. This will help to reinforce this concept and get students to practice using positive words on a more frequent basis.

Give the students an example of a word that fits under each list to get them thinking in the correct direction.

ADDITIONAL RESOURCES:

Online sources of negative and positive words that are commonly used.

Vocab Makeover
NEGATIVE SIDE

DIRECTIONS: Select six negative words and place them in the negative "cause" boxes. In the two negative "effects" boxes, for each one, list two effects that using the negative word could possibly have on a person.

CAUSE **EFFECTS** (NEGATIVE)

NEGATIVE WORDS

| can't | Give up without trying very hard. |
| | Feel like a failure. |

| should | Feel like I have to do what others want me to (peers). |
| | Makes me feel guilty or disloyal if I don't. |

| might | Lowers my confidence. |
| | Lowers my effort level. |

| lazy | Makes me feel like not trying. |
| | Why bother then? |

| impossible | I quit trying. |
| | I feel like a failure. |

| fail | I have little value. |
| | Creates self doubt and I feel like a loser. |

(continued)

Vocab Makeover
POSITIVE SIDE

DIRECTIONS: Select six positive words and place them in the positive "cause" boxes. In the two positive "effects" boxes, for each one, list two effects that using the positive word could possibly have on a person.

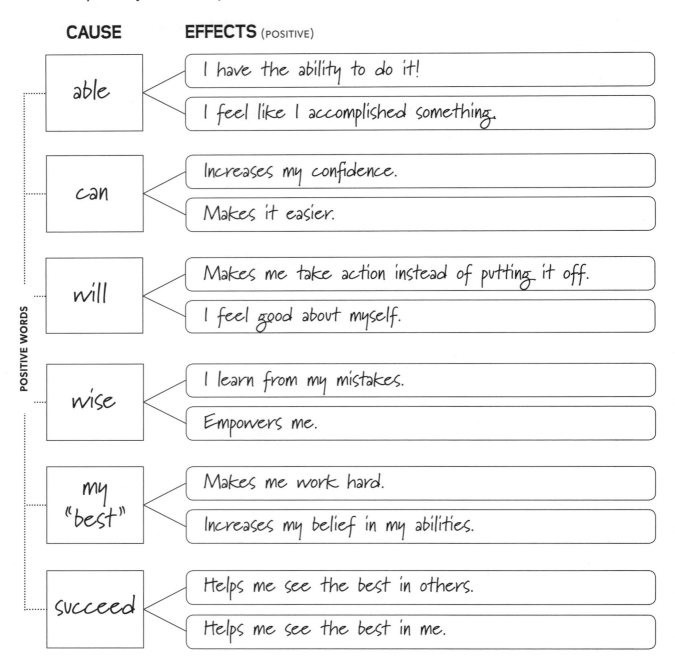

CAUSE   **EFFECTS** (POSITIVE)

POSITIVE WORDS

able
- I have the ability to do it!
- I feel like I accomplished something.

can
- Increases my confidence.
- Makes it easier.

will
- Makes me take action instead of putting it off.
- I feel good about myself.

wise
- I learn from my mistakes.
- Empowers me.

my "best"
- Makes me work hard.
- Increases my belief in my abilities.

succeed
- Helps me see the best in others.
- Helps me see the best in me.

Get Creative!

OBJECTIVES:

Social Skills: Students will display the ability to concentrate on the task they are working on.

Executive Functions: Students will exhibit self-control by concentrating on a task without being distracted.

MATERIALS NEEDED:

- Paper
- Pencil
- Computer access
- Poster board and glue (if making the vision boards without computers, see steps 1 and 2 below)
- Newspapers and magazines (if making the vision boards without computers, see steps 1 and 2 below)
- Boys Town Social Skill poster, "Concentrating on a Subject or Task"

Students can promote positive thinking by engaging in creative projects. For this activity, students will create vision boards to help them stay focused on goals. You may need to explain the concept of vision boards to students. Vision boards are visual reminders of affirmations or goals. Some believe that vision boards help clarify, allow you to concentrate, and keep a person focused on a larger goal.

TEACHER INSTRUCTIONS:

1. **Prior to class,** decide whether you will create an online vision board or have students create a vision board using poster board and magazines.

2. If using poster board and magazines, collect the necessary items and make them accessible to students.

3. If using an online vision board website, select a website that allows you to create online vision boards for free (such as picmonkey.com, visionboardme. com, dreamitalive.com, or Pinterest). As a note, Visionboardme.com and Picmonkey.com are both easy to use. PicMonkey.com allows you to add text.

Be certain to prompt students about appropriate use of the Internet, and monitor their activities if accessing online tools.

4. **During class,** ask students to reflect on their dreams, goals, and what makes them happy. Suggest they write down several ideas they have on a piece of paper. DREAM BIG!

5. Inform the students they will be creating their own vision boards. (Explain the purpose of a vision board if necessary.)

6. Explain to students that in order to be successful, they will need to ignore distractions and concentrate. Review the steps of the Boys Town Social Skill **Concentrating on a Subject or Task**:
   a. *Promptly begin work on the task.*
   b. *Focus your attention directly on the subject.*
   c. *If your attention wanders, instruct yourself to concentrate on the task.*
   d. *Ignore distractions or interruptions by others.*
   e. *Remain on-task until the work is completed.*

7. Instruct students to start collecting images and inspirational, positive sayings to put in the collage.

8. Give students time to complete their vision boards.

9. Share the vision boards with the class by:
   a. Displaying the vision boards on a projector or SmartBoard;
   b. Printing the vision boards and displaying them; or
   c. Hanging the poster board products in the room.

10. Provide time for students to present their boards to the group. Encourage students to talk about their dreams and goals, but also respect the private nature of dreams and goals of some students.

11. Encourage students to display their vision boards outside of class in a prominent place that might help them stay focused.

Visit several of the online vision board sites to see which you prefer. Make a personal vision board to share with the students.

FLIPPED CLASSROOM:

Instruct students to make an online vision board to share with the class.

ADDITIONAL RESOURCES:

Free, online vision board sites.

LOL!

OBJECTIVES:

Social Skills: Students will practice using appropriate humor in the classroom.

Executive Functions: Students will display zest by showing enthusiasm in the exploration of laughter and humor.

MATERIALS NEEDED:

- Paper
- Pencil
- Assortment of cartoons, riddles, funny pictures, etc.
- Large index cards for making a class set of "different laughs" cards
- Markers
- Access to computers or other devices for Internet use
- Dictionaries (if not using online sources)
- Boys Town Social Skill poster, "Using Appropriate Humor"

 Laughter triggers positive thinking and can give an individual a more optimistic perspective when faced with problems, stress, and difficult situations. Laughter gives us more energy and is a contagious happiness that can be shared between individuals.

TEACHER INSTRUCTIONS:

1. **Prior to class,** make a class set of "different laughs" cards. Large index cards work well for this. Think of as many different types of laughs as possible and print each one on a separate card. The Internet is a good source for this. Here are a few to get you started: giggle, snicker, chuckle, snort, cackle, chortle, roar, guffaw, etc.

2. **During class,** set the tone of the lesson by providing students with cartoons, riddles, funny pictures, etc., to look at as they enter the classroom. Give them a few minutes to read, chuckle, and share with others.

3. Distribute a "different laughs" card to each student. Provide time for them to search for the meaning of their card's type of laugh online or through the use of dictionaries.

4. Ask each student to demonstrate their type of laugh to the class. Have fun with this!

5. Assign as homework the task to find a funny story, joke, picture, or riddle to share with the class the next day. Hold a competition for the most funny.

6. Remind students of the importance of **Using Appropriate Humor** by:
   a. *Using humor only under appropriate circumstances.*
   b. *Avoiding humor that makes fun of groups in society, disabled people, or individuals in your peer group.*
   c. *Avoid sexually-oriented jokes and profanity.*
   d. *If humor does offend others, be ready to promptly and sincerely apologize.*

7. Make sure the students know you will have to approve each joke, story, picture, or riddle before they can present them to the class.

Make sure all humor found and used is classroom appropriate.

FLIPPED CLASSROOM:

Prior to class, ask the students to find at least ten different types of laughs and define each one. Instruct them to write each one on an index card with the definition on the back of the card. Bring to class.

Turning Problems into Opportunities

Sometimes all we need is a little perspective... a little "different" perspective. Students need to realize problems are really just opportunities to find new solutions, try something different, or do something in a different way. Recognizing and being able to use various problem-solving strategies helps a child become successful. Half of the battle lies in the ability to accurately define the problem. Problem-solving strategies are skills that can be learned and improved upon.

Another key component to problem-solving is continuing to work at the problem until it is resolved or solved. It is through grit and perseverance that we become successful in gaining autonomy in problem-solving. Students also need opportunities to practice applying problem-solving strategies just as one might need to spend time practicing for an athletic or musical competition.

Setbacks and frustrations are a normal part of turning problems into opportunities and should be seen as obstacles that can be overcome and do not need to become permanent. It is okay to fail at something, but it is not okay to get "stuck" there. Our failures need to be turned into golden nuggets of learning.

Activities included in this section are:
- Lemons to Lemonade
- Defining the Problem
- Different Perspectives
- Flip/Flop!
- Try, Try Again

Lemons to Lemonade

OBJECTIVES:

Social Skills: Students will contribute to the group activity using optimism.

Executive Functions: Students will cultivate optimism by finding positive ways to state problems.

MATERIALS NEEDED:

- Paper
- Pencil
- 5-6 lemons (dependent on class size). Keep one whole, but cut the rest into slices for each of the students to taste.
- Lemonade
- Pitcher
- Small cups
- Access to tablets or mobile devices
- (Optional, see step 14) Problem-solving apps such as "iMazing" and "Where's My Water?"
- Boys Town Social Skill poster, "Expressing Optimism"

It is important to emphasize the importance of training our mind to see the opportunities in problems. Seeing the opportunities gives students hope and confidence they can overcome their difficulties.

TEACHER INSTRUCTIONS:

1. **Prior to class,** make a pitcher of lemonade and slice the lemons.

2. **During class,** distribute a slice of lemon to each of the students.

3. Ask students to taste the lemon and describe the taste. Many will say "sour" or they "don't like the taste" and they are too hard to eat.

4. Explain how the lemons will represent the problems they face in life. Just like lemons, we don't like problems and think they are too hard to solve. We only see the lemon! (Problem)

5. Ask students to tell you how you could turn lemons into something better or tastier. (Lemonade, lemon pie, etc.)

6. Offer each student a small cup of lemonade.

7. Discuss with students:
    a. Ask if this tastes better than the lemon? *(Most will say yes.)*
    b. Ask how lemonade is made and what ingredients are used? *(Sugar and water)*
    c. Explain how the lemonade represents opportunities in life and by taking our problems, the lemons, and changing them a little (adding in sugar and water) we can provide opportunities (lemonade).
    d. Explain to students that problems are really just opportunities to find new solutions, try something different, or do something in a different way. It might end up being better than they can even imagine. When we focus on trying to find solutions instead of just the problem, then the mind finds opportunities. If a problem is stated in a more exciting way, it is easier to focus on the opportunities.

8. Divide the class into groups of two or three.

9. Explain to the class that for the next part of the activity they will need to practice using the Boys Town Social Skill **Expressing Optimism**. Promoting optimism will help students create positive ways of stating problems. The steps are:
    a. *Look at your group.*
    b. *Use an enthusiastic voice tone.*
    c. *Describe potential positive outcomes.*
    d. *Express hope and desire for positive outcomes.*
    e. *Thank the group for listening.*

10. Ask students to brainstorm other problems (lemons) like this that can be turned into opportunities (Lemonade).

11. Spend time practicing how to state the problem in a more positive way. Each group should try four or five. (Example: "My locker is always jammed" into "I'm going to think of ways to open my locker easily." The second way offers more opportunities.)

12. After the activity is complete, have the students share examples with the class.

13. Post the ideas somewhere in the classroom where students will be reminded to state a problem in a more positive manner.

14. If time permits, allow the students to explore some apps that make problem-solving fun. "iMazing" and "Where's My Water?" are a few. These are free downloads that can be put on a tablet or mobile device.

 Check for food allergies before starting this lesson. Arrange for access to Tablets or other mobile devices if using step 14.

FLIPPED CLASSROOM:
Explore problem-solving apps prior to coming to class.

ADDITIONAL RESOURCES:
Various problem-solving apps.

Defining the Problem

OBJECTIVES:

Social Skills: Students will improve their ability to define problems. They will also ask for clarification when needed in an appropriate way.

Executive Functions: Students will practice self-control by paying attention and getting to work right away. By asking questions to deepen understanding, students will also display curiosity.

MATERIALS NEEDED:

- Paper
- Pencil
- Defining the problem quote by Albert Einstein (see step 1)
- "Defining the Problem" worksheet
- Boys Town Social Skill poster, "Using Structured Problem Solving (SODAS)"
- Boys Town Social Skill poster, "Asking For Clarification"

 It is important to teach students how to properly identify a problem. Without precisely knowing what the problem is, how can a person ever succeed in solving it?

TEACHER INSTRUCTIONS:

1. **Prior to class,** post the following quote by Albert Einstein somewhere in the classroom:

   "If I had only one hour to save the world, I would spend fifty-five minutes defining the problem and only five minutes finding that solution."

2. **During class,** present the quote to students and discuss: What did Albert Einstein mean by this quote?

3. List several ideas that the students have on the board. Eventually arrive at the notion he felt it was extremely important to define and understand what the problem is before you can hope to solve it.

4. Tell students the Boys Town Social Skill **Using Structured Problem Solving (SODAS)** also states it is important to define the problem. Review the following five steps to solving problems with the students:

    a. Define the problem situation.
    b. Generate two or more options.
    c. Look at each option's potential disadvantage.
    d. Look at each option's potential advantages.
    e. Decide on the best solution.

Remind students this structure can be used on any problem.

5. Distribute the "Defining the Problem" worksheet to individual students or student pairs, providing the following instructions:

    a. Students will state what the original problem is.
    b. Students will have two squares to further identify or describe the problem. This is important so they better understand what the problem is stating.
    c. Students will have three squares to rephrase the problem. By rephrasing the problem, students can find better ways of writing the problem that will ultimately generate more possible solutions.
    d. Students will have one square to say what the problem "is not." This step will further identify the specific problem.
    e. Lastly, there will be a square for writing the problem in a positive way. (See activity "Lemons to Lemonade" for more ideas on this.)

6. Explain to the students this might seem difficult or confusing if they have never approached a problem like this before. If they are struggling, remind them of the steps of the Boys Town Social Skill **Asking for Clarification**:

    a. Look at the person.
    b. Ask if he or she has time to talk. Don't interrupt.
    c. Use a pleasant or neutral tone of voice.
    d. Specifically state what you are confused about. Begin with "I was wondering if…" or "Could I ask about…?"
    e. Listen to the other person's reply and acknowledge the answer.
    f. Thank the person for his or her time.

Defining the Problem

DIRECTIONS: Read the following sentences carefully and answer by filling in the blanks or writing in the space provided. Please use complete sentences.

STATE THE ORIGINAL PROBLEM

I feel disorganized.

or

I have a problem with organization of my supplies.

Further identify or describe the problem to better understand what the problem is stating.

IDENTIFY   I can't find my assignments.
I don't have what I need for class.

DESCRIBE   My locker is a mess and I don't know what to do with all my papers.

Rephrase the problem three different ways. This will help generate more possible solutions.

1
How do I organize my papers?

2
Is there a way to keep my locker clean?

3
Where is the best place to keep my assignments?

State what the problem "is not" (also called "reversing it"). This step will further identify the specific problem.

The problem is not feeling organized.

The problem is not that I don't know how to do my homework.

WRITE THE PROBLEM IN A POSITIVE WAY

I have an opportunity to create a way of keeping all my papers in a place I can find them to help me succeed.

Different Perspectives

OBJECTIVES:

Social Skills: Students will understand and apply the use of rationales when formulating varying perspectives.

Executive Functions: Students will practice social intelligence by being able to see a problem or situation from another's perspective.

MATERIALS NEEDED:

- Paper
- Pencil
- YouTube video "Different Perspectives" (see steps 1 and 3)
- Ability to project or display video for the class
- Whiteboard or chalkboard
- Writing utensil for the board
- Sample of M.C. Escher's work ("Day and Night" and "Sky and Water" are great examples, see step 6)
- "Different Perspectives" worksheet
- Insanity quote by Albert Einstein (see step 13)
- Boys Town Social Skill poster, "Giving Rationales"

 In learning to define problems, it is important to view them from different perspectives because that increases the possible solutions. Viewpoint adds innovation.

TEACHER INSTRUCTIONS:

1. **Prior to class,** locate the YouTube video titled "Different Perspectives" (https://www.youtube.com/watch?v=rGiTDdTC-fY). Have the video available to show to students.

2. **During class,** review the previous lesson on defining problems:

a. Ask for volunteers to restate the different ways used for understanding a problem better.

b. Make sure to touch on describing the problem, rephrasing it two or three times, saying what it is not, and stating it in a positive way.

c. Remind students this is a successful strategy to solving a number of problems.

3. Show the YouTube video "Different Perspectives." (It is only 23 seconds long.)

4. Ask students to rephrase what they think the video message is.

5. Write all ideas on the board. Eventually state the video emphasizes the ability to shift our perspective in order to see a problem or situation differently.

6. Show students the work of the artist, M.C. Escher. "Day and Night" and "Sky and Water" are two pieces of his work that show how perspective can help us to see things differently. You can find his work online or in art books.

7. Explain the importance of viewing problems from multiple perspectives to the students and discuss:

a. Being able to see problems from different perspectives allows them the ability to look at situations from different angles. You can see it close up or far away, or from behind someone, etc.

b. The way we see some problem or situation can give us information, or it can be a hindrance to our ability to see possible solutions.

c. Ask students to share a time when something happened at school and different people had different perspectives of the incident.

d. It is important to be able to change our perspective because it unleashes our creativity and reveals something unexpected or different.

e. It is also advantageous to be able to see problems or situations from the viewpoint of others. Would a teacher and a student see things the same? How about a boy and a girl? A rich person or a poor person? A tall person or a short person? Each different perspective can offer additional insight and creative solutions to a problem or situation we might not even be aware of.

8. Divide the students into groups of three.

9. Give each group a copy of the "Different Perspectives" worksheet, explaining that each problem or question needs to be answered from the perspective of the person or groups of people on the list. For instance on the question, "What do students need in order to be successful in school?"

    a. A person living in poverty might answer "food."
    b. A high school senior might say, "To study hard and go to class."
    c. An adult might say, "Listen to the teacher and do your work," etc.

10. While working with their group, students might need to give their rationale for the perspectives they are supposed to write. Review the steps of the Boys Town Social Skill **Giving Rationales**:

    a. *Look at the person or people in your group.*
    b. *Explain your point-of-view with rationales the other person or people can understand.*
    c. *Use rationales that point out the potential benefit to the other person(s).*
    d. *Ask if the person or group understands your reasoning.*

11. Provide students time to complete the activity.

12. Once the activity is complete, review and discuss the answers as a class, emphasizing the importance of being able to look at problems and situations from many perspectives in order to be more efficient in solving and dealing with them.

13. Explain to students that Albert Einstein is quoted to have said, "Insanity is doing the same thing over and over again and expecting different results."

14. Ask students to write down on a piece of paper how this quote relates to problem-solving and perspective. *(Answer: If we only try solving our problems by doing the same thing over and over, that is insanity. We need different perspectives that lead to trying other solutions.)*

15. Use these as an exit pass for the students. Post this quote as a reminder for the students.

Collect samples of M.C. Escher's work to show the students. It's easiest to bookmark the two suggested pieces of art on your computer.

FLIPPED CLASSROOM:

Instruct students to watch the following YouTube video:
https://www.youtube.com/watch?v=rGiTDdTC-fY

Ask them to write a paragraph on the meaning of the video and bring it to class. Collect the paragraphs as an entrance pass to the class, then proceed with the rest of the lesson.

ADDITIONAL RESOURCES:

Examples of M.C. Escher's work

ACTIVITY

Different Perspectives

DIRECTIONS: Answer each question based on the perspective of the person listed.

PROBLEM #1   **What technology should be used in the classroom?**

Senior citizen: <u>Books and computer; others might say the latest technology</u>

Person living in Poverty: <u>Mobile phones or whatever is available</u>

Six-year-old: <u>iPod and apps</u>

Teacher: <u>Anything available that motivates and prepares students</u>

High School Student: <u>Phones, tablets, computers, social networking</u>

Bill Gates: <u>Microsoft!</u>

Person from 3rd world country: <u>Any that's available. Radio, digital camera, digital drum (Uganda)</u>

PROBLEM #2   **What is the best food to serve students for lunch?**

Middle school student: <u>Pizza, fruit snacks</u>

Parent: <u>Good, healthy food</u>

Doctor: <u>Fruits, vegetables and lean proteins</u>

Soft drink supplier: <u>Soda pop! Soda pop! Soda pop!</u>

High School Student: <u>Fast food, salads</u>

4th-grader: <u>Chicken nuggets, lunchables, fruit snacks</u>

Nutrition expert: <u>A nutritious balanced meal</u>

PROBLEM #3   **What do students need to be successful in school?**

Adult: <u>To study hard; focus, determination</u>

High school graduate: <u>Know how to take tests; time management</u>

Politician: <u>Communication skills</u>

Business owner: <u>Knowledge of the "market"; be able to work in teams</u>

Manufacturing worker: <u>Skills for the job market</u>

Person living on low income: <u>Help from teachers when needed, grit</u>

Teacher: <u>Motivation, good attitude, grit</u>

Flip/Flop!

OBJECTIVES:

Social Skills: Students will develop good quality work while understanding problems.

Executive Functions: Students will have the opportunity to develop their curiosity by exploring new ways of understanding problems.

MATERIALS NEEDED:

- Paper
- Pencil
- "Reflections on Problem Solving" worksheet
- Several envelopes (at least three per group)
- Problems for the envelopes
- Container for the envelopes
- Boys Town Social Skill poster, "Doing Good Quality Work"
- Possible prizes for the team with the most points.

TEACHER INSTRUCTIONS:

1. **Prior to class,** prepare several envelopes that contain a single problem (see Additional Resources for ideas).

2. **During class,** review the prior three lessons on problem-solving by giving each student a copy of the "Reflections on Problem Solving" worksheet.

3. Provide time for students to reflect on what they have learned about problem-solving so far.

4. Discuss as a class and encourage students to add to their worksheets, as they need to.

5. Explain to students they have some great resources now for solving problems, but sometimes it is still hard to come up with solutions. This next strategy helps with this dilemma. Students will use the principle of "flip/flop" or reversing the problem.

6. Divide students into groups and provide the following instructions:

    a. Ask each group to select an envelope from the container.

    b. Read the problem in the envelope.

    c. After reading the problem in the envelope they must write down the "flip/flop" or reverse of the problem. (See examples in Additional Resources.) So, if the problem in the envelope was "how to get better grades", the reverse would be "how to get worse grades."

    d. As a team they will find solutions to the reverse problem. (Example: Don't do homework, or don't pay attention to instructions, etc.)

    e. Once they have as many solutions as they can think of to the reverse problem, they will show it to you and you will reward one point for each legitimate solution.

7. This is a good time to remind students of the importance of doing good quality work. If the solutions are not good quality they will not receive a point. Review the Boys Town Social Skill **Doing Good Quality Work**:

    a. Find out the exact expectations or instructions for tasks.

    b. Assemble the necessary tools or materials.

    c. Carefully begin working. Focus your attention on the task.

    d. Continue working until the task is completed or criteria are met.

    e. Examine the results of your work to make sure it was done correctly.

    f. Correct any deficiencies, if necessary. Perhaps, check back with the person who assigned the task.

8. Instruct students to take all of the reverse problem solutions and now flip/flop those to make solutions for the original problem.

9. Have students share their solutions. Award two points for each legitimate solution. (Example: Do homework and pay attention to instructions, etc.)

 Make the problems relevant to the issues your students face.

ADDITIONAL RESOURCES:

List of possible problems:

    a. How do I get better grades?

    b. How do I find my cell phone?

    c. How do I get my locker open?

    d. How to keep from cheating?

    e. How to find answers to homework?

    f. How to get work turned in on time?

Reflections on Problem Solving

DIRECTIONS: Complete each section. Provide three ideas in each section.

what did I learn about turning problems into opportunities?

I learned that problems might appear difficult at first but breaking them down (chunking) makes them easier to solve.

Gives me opportunities to do something different or better.

If I keep working, I will eventually change or resolve the problem.

Why is it important to look at problems from different perspectives?

It generates or promotes my brain to think of different solutions by thinking of the problem in different ways.

Albert Einstein said he would spend 55 minutes defining a problem and 5 minutes finding a solution. What strategies have we learned about better identifying problems?

Describe it.

Rephrase it.

Look at it from different perspectives.

Say what it is not.

See the problem as an opportunity.

Chunk them.

Try, Try Again

OBJECTIVES:

Social Skills: Students will understand the importance of persevering on tasks and projects.

Executive Functions: Students will show grit by continuing to work on solutions to problems.

MATERIALS NEEDED:

- Paper
- Pencil
- "Chunk It" worksheet
- Boys Town Social Skill poster, "Persevering on Tasks and Projects"

One of the most important aspects to be learned from attempting to solve a problem is to continue working at it until it is resolved. We don't always get the solution right away, but rather we must try, try, again. It is okay to fail, so don't pretend it doesn't happen. Help students acknowledge the setback or frustration and formulate a way to move past it.

TEACHER INSTRUCTIONS:

1. Remind students of all the ways covered to define a problem and look for solutions. Emphasize that even when they have tried all of those strategies they still may not have a solution. It is important they continue to try and not give up.

2. Teach students the Boys Town Social Skill **Persevering on Tasks and Projects**:
   a. *Know exactly what must be done in order to complete a task or project. (In this case, know what must be done to solve a problem.)*
   b. *Get started promptly without procrastinating.*

       c. *Remain on task until finished.*
       d. *Deal appropriately with frustrations or disappointments.*

3. Distribute the "Chunk It" worksheets to students, providing the following instructions:
       a. Explain to students another problem-solving strategy is to find what the problem is a part of.
       b. Ask, are there little parts that make up the whole problem? Compare this to parts of a pizza. The slices are parts to the whole.

4. Pose the following problem to the students:

"Failing a test." (You could also pose a problem you have had in the classroom.)

5. Ask students to identify as many little parts to this problem as possible. They want to find out why they failed the test. These are a few examples of questions or chunks they might ask.
       a. Why did this happen?
       b. What was it about the test that was hard?
       c. Did I fail to do something prior to the test?

6. Ask students to split their circle into pieces; one for each chunk they can think of. Try at least five or six.

7. After students have identified their pieces or chunks, have them write answers to these chunking questions to help them better understand the problem. In doing this, they will often find the solution to the problem.

8. Discuss suggestions and findings with the class.

FLIPPED CLASSROOM:
Ask students to come to class with a definition of "chunking a problem" and how it is beneficial. Discuss in class as part of step 2 under Teacher Instructions.

ACTIVITY

Chunk It

DIRECTIONS: After identifying little parts to the problem, split the circle into pieces. Each piece represents a chunk of the problem you can think of. Try at least five or six. After identifying the chunks, write an answer to each of the chunking questions.

PROBLEM I failed a test.

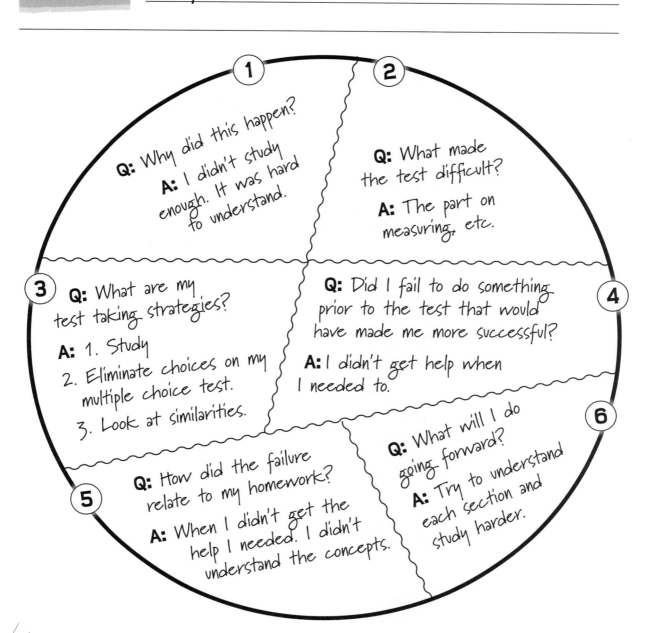

1 **Q:** Why did this happen? **A:** I didn't study enough. It was hard to understand.

2 **Q:** What made the test difficult? **A:** The part on measuring, etc.

3 **Q:** What are my test taking strategies? **A:** 1. Study 2. Eliminate choices on my multiple choice test. 3. Look at similarities.

4 **Q:** Did I fail to do something prior to the test that would have made me more successful? **A:** I didn't get help when I needed to.

5 **Q:** How did the failure relate to my homework? **A:** When I didn't get the help I needed. I didn't understand the concepts.

6 **Q:** What will I do going forward? **A:** Try to understand each section and study harder.

SECTION 5

You've Got This!
From Rescue to Personal Autonomy

Learning from our failures and struggles gives us valuable insight for solving future problems that will arise. Students need to believe in their abilities to find solutions for the problems they face. They don't always need the "life preserver." Sometimes all they need is a little encouragement and self-confidence in order to see themselves as being capable of overcoming obstacles and difficulties. We want our students to believe they have the skills to successfully navigate their life when facing challenges.

Learning to effectively solve problems is a lifelong skill that provides opportunities to grow, learn, and create new and different solutions. Remember, problems are a constant, real fact of life everyone must confront. If we teach our youth how to effectively approach

and solve problems, we are helping them to develop lifelong critical thinking abilities that will help them focus on the opportunities instead of "drowning" under the weight of their problems.

Activities included in this section are:

- I Wouldn't Do That Again!
- Life Preserver or Not? A Work in Progress
- Action!
- Connect the Dots

START
1 Problem
Rephrase It 2
3 Say It Positive
What It Isn't 4
5 Possible Solutions
6 Solution

I Wouldn't Do That Again!

OBJECTIVES:

Social Skills: Students will understand there are positive ways of dealing with failure, and mistakes are an important and necessary step to success.

Executive Functions: Students will recognize trying hard after a mistake or failure is a sign of having grit.

MATERIALS NEEDED:

- Paper
- Pencil
- YouTube videos on famous failures or making mistakes (see step 1)
- "I Wouldn't Do That Again" worksheet
- Boys Town Social Skill poster, "Dealing With Failure"

 Autonomy in making decisions is necessary to build confidence in problem-solving abilities. Learning from failures and struggles gives valuable insight for future problem-solving attempts. Understanding what doesn't work is an important and necessary step towards success.

TEACHER INSTRUCTIONS:

1. **Prior to class,** locate 2-3 Famous Failures or Making Mistakes videos. Here are two examples:
    https://www.youtube.com/watch?v=45mMioJ5szc
    https://www.youtube.com/watch?v=Oh42WIdyHUw

2. **During class,** begin by showing the 2-3 Famous Failures or Making Mistakes videos to the class.

3. Give students a few minutes to discuss with a partner the meaning of the videos. Share the responses with the class.

4. Point out that mistakes are a normal and necessary part of life that can eventually lead to success, if we allow them to. Self-confidence is built when one can problem solve past a mistake.

5. Instruct students to, after class, interview five people about mistakes they have made and will not repeat. Students should ask questions such as:
   a. What was the mistake?
   b. Did you learn anything from it? If so, what?
   c. Did this mistake eventually lead you to success? If so, how?

6. Ask students to write an online summary of what they learned from these five people about mistakes. Google Docs works well for this. You can use another online document system if you choose.

7. Distribute the "I Wouldn't Do That Again" worksheet to each student, instructing them to reflect on one of their own mistakes and answer the questions on the worksheet.

8. Post students' responses in the room as a reminder that it is okay to make mistakes when attempting to solve problems.

9. Some students may experience difficulty accepting they have failed or made a mistake. Stress the importance of learning from mistakes in order to be more successful. Take the time to review the steps to **Dealing with Failure** with students:
   a. *Accurately identify you did not succeed in a particular activity.*
   b. *Remain calm and relaxed.*
   c. *Instruct yourself to control emotional behavior.*
   d. *Find a caring adult and discuss your disappointment or other negative feelings.*
   e. *Be willing to try again to be successful.*

Check to make sure all "I Wouldn't Do That Again" examples are appropriate for sharing before posting.

FLIPPED CLASSROOM:

View two YouTube videos on making mistakes. (See above.) Write a review of each one. Assign students to interview five people about mistakes they've made and write an online summary of what these people learned from their mistakes. (See step 4 for sample questions.)

ADDITIONAL RESOURCES:

Various YouTube videos of famous failures. It would also be helpful to have a list of adults in your building who would be willing to share a mistake experience with a student who doesn't have five resources.

I Wouldn't Do That Again

DIRECTIONS: Reflect on one of your mistakes and answer the questions below.

My biggest mistake is: _____

One time I had a big project due. We were supposed to have been working on it for weeks. I didn't start it until the night before it was due. I had to stay up all night to work on it. I felt physically sick while presenting it to the class the next day. I received a poor grade.

What I learned: _____

I learned to have and practice better time management.
I learned to not procrastinate.
I learned to chunk the parts of a project.
I learned to not stay up all night when you have to make a presentation.

Why I wouldn't do that again: _I could have done better if_
I would have spent more time on the project, but instead I got
a bad grade.

I don't like feeling sick.

Did any success result from this mistake? If so, what?
Yes. I realized that I have to allow for the time it will take to
produce a project.

I have better time management skills and I don't procrastinate
as much.

How will I use this mistake to better myself or make myself more successful?
I will not put off big tasks until the very end.

I realized that I am capable of more if I put forth
the effort.

Life Preserver or Not?
A Work in Progress

OBJECTIVES:

Social Skills: Students will set a goal of how to solve a problem they are facing.

Executive Functions: Students will exhibit grit while trying to find solutions to various problems.

MATERIALS NEEDED:

- 8 ½" x 5 ½" pieces of paper (at least five per student)
- Pencil
- Scissors
- WikiHow on Passing Your Body through a Sheet of Paper (see steps 1 and 9)
- "A Work in Progress Plan of Action" worksheet
- Boys Town Social Skill poster, "Setting Goals"

 One of the obstacles to effective problem-solving is a student's belief about his or her own ability to succeed. Helping a student see the many possible solutions to problems builds hope and increases their chance of success. Allowing time to practice effective problem-solving strategies through problem-solving goal setting helps youth to realize they don't always need the "life preserver." Sometimes they can "swim to shore."

TEACHER INSTRUCTIONS:

1. **Prior to class,** locate the WikiHow: http://www.wikihow.com/Pass-Your-Body-Through-a-Sheet-of-Paper.
   Be able to display it for the class in step 9 or print and distribute.

2. Cut a large hole in an 8½" x 5½" piece of paper for demonstration (see step 3).

3. **During class,** show students an 8½" x 5½" piece of paper with a large hole cut in it. Tell them you have been trying to cut the paper with a hole large enough for you to fit your body through it, without ripping the paper.

4. Show students how this is not working. Tell them you need help in figuring out the problem.

5. Give each student an 8½" x 5½" piece of paper and provide an additional stack of extra papers for the students to have access to in case they need more than one.

6. Provide time for the students to experiment with trying to cut the paper in ways that it produces a hole large enough for your body to pass through without ripping the paper. Most students will not be able to do this.

7. Ask if anyone successfully solved this problem? Discuss the answers.

8. Point out the first piece of paper you showed them, with the large hole, represented the way most people look at problems. They only look at it from one way and therefore have a very small chance of finding a solution. Explain when the students were experimenting, they were approaching the problem from many different perspectives. That is an important part to successfully being able to solve our own problems; however sometimes we still don't see a solution.

9. Show students the following Wikihow tutorial on how to cut the paper so your body can pass through. (Make sure you practice this before showing the students.)
http://www.wikihow.com/Pass-Your-Body-Through-a-Sheet-of-Paper

Emphasize that by making cuts in the paper that one wouldn't normally consider, it is possible to pass a person's body through it without ripping the edges.

10. Distribute a copy of the "A Work in Progress Plan of Action" worksheet to each student.

11. Ask students to think of a current problem they are facing and record it in the blank provided on the worksheet.

12. This is a good time to discuss goal-setting. Being able to set a goal and work towards it builds confidence in students. Review the Boys Town Social Skill **Setting Goals** with students and then post in the classroom:
    a. *Decide on your overall values and lifestyle desires.*
       (Problem and Dream It steps on the "A Work In Progress Plan of Action" worksheet)

b.   *List the resources you need to fulfill these lifestyle options.*
(Plan It step on the worksheet)

c.   *Examine the intermediate steps in accomplishing your overall outcome.*
(Work It step on the worksheet)

d.   *Establish short–and long-term goals that will help you accomplish the steps necessary for the desired outcome.*
(Work It and Endure It steps on the worksheet)

13. Review each step of the worksheet with the students. Provide time to complete. Stress the importance of not always needing to take the "life preserver" but rather to take the steps necessary to solve many of their own problems.

Try Teacher Instruction steps 1-6 on your own prior to class.
Make a sample to show the students.

A Work in Progress Plan of Action

DIRECTIONS: Use the following steps to make a plan for successfully solving a problem.

WHAT	ACTION PLAN
(1) THE PROBLEM *Describe it.*	I got a "C" on my last science test. I want an A or B on the next one.
(2) PLAN IT *Practice the strategies of defining the problem, i.e. the restating, "chucking," say opposite, etc.*	Reverse It: I want a worse grade. Rephrase: I didn't study hard for my science test. Describe: I struggle with the Science concepts that are taught.
(3) WORK IT *What are the working plan of steps needed to solve the problem? What are the short and long term steps?*	I will "Chunk it" — break the sections down. I will study 15 minutes every night reviewing the science learned that day. If I do not understand, I will arrange a time with the teacher to get help. I will start studying for tests five days prior.
(4) ENDURE IT *What obstacles might you face and how will you handle those?*	Distractions: Remove myself to some place quiet. Procrastination: No other activity until homework is finished. Not understanding: Seek help.
(5) OWN IT *Did you have the solution and was it the outcome you expected? If no, describe how it changed.*	Yes! I improved!!

Action!

OBJECTIVES:

Social Skills: Students will create a problem-solving visual message by carefully selecting the appropriate words to use for the greatest impact.

Executive Functions: Students will practice self-control by allowing others to contribute and promptly beginning their work.

MATERIALS NEEDED:

- Paper
- Pencils
- Whiteboard or chalkboard
- Examples of short videos such as Animotos, 15-second Instagrams, and 6-second Vines (these are different programs used in making short, impactful, digital video messages, see steps 1 and 5)
- Access to computers, iPads, Tablets, or other devices
- Boys Town Social Skill poster, "Choosing Appropriate Words"

TEACHER INSTRUCTIONS:

1. **Prior to class,** research and locate examples of short videos such as Animotos, 15-second Instagrams or 6-second Vines. Choose examples that have strong messages in their short times. Be prepared to be able demonstrate these for the class.

2. Ensure the technology to be used in class has the appropriate social media applications downloaded (Animoto, Instragram or Vine).

3. **During class,** explain to students being able to solve problems independently contributes to healthy self-esteem. It builds confidence in being able to obtain success when faced with a problem or challenge.

4. Ask students to list five things they have learned about improving their ability to solve problems. Write the list on the board.

5. Explain to students messages can be brief while still packing an impactful "punch". Show a few short video examples (using the Animotos, Instagrams, and Vine videos selected prior to class).

6. Divide the class into groups of two or three. (Students could work individually, as well.)

7. Explain to students they will be using the list on the board, or an individual list, to compose a message about how other people can solve their own problems. Encourage them to use several of the strategies they have explored.

8. Explain words are powerful and have the ability to influence people. Emphasize the importance of choosing the appropriate words for the message they are sending. Show them the Boys Town Social Skill **Choosing Appropriate Words**:
   a. *Look at the situation around you.*
   b. *Know the meaning of the words you are about to say/write.*
   c. *Refrain from using words that will offend people around you or that they will not understand.*
   d. *Avoid using slang, profanity, or words that could have sexual meaning.*
   e. *Decide what thought you want to put into words then say/write the words.*

9. Have each group (or student) spend time composing a Problem Solving Message.

10. After the groups have composed the messages and have checked for word appropriateness, ask them to produce their message in the form of an Animoto, a 15-second Instagram, or a 6-second Vine message.

(Music can be added to these programs if desired.)

11. Share the messages with the school in a commons area or post them to your class or school website/blog for others to view.

Emphasize the messages should be brief but impactful. If you are not familiar with how to use the apps in this activity, there are very simple instructions available on the Internet or in the Help sections of the apps themselves.

FLIPPED CLASSROOM:

Assign students to view an Animoto, 15-second Instagram, and 6-second Vine before coming to class. Ask them to choose the one they will use to produce their message, and to write and bring a rough draft of the message to the next class. Another option would be to create the entire Problem Solving Message prior to class and then share the messages during class time.

ADDITIONAL RESOURCES:

Online video creating programs.

Connect the Dots

OBJECTIVES:

Social Skills: Students will be able to identify several effective strategies to use when problem-solving.

Executive Functions: Students will show grit and self-control by paying attention and working independently.

MATERIALS NEEDED:

- Card stock (9" x 12")
- Scratch paper (a few pages per student)
- Pencil
- Crayons, colored pencils, etc.
- Various "Connect the Dots" worksheets (free worksheets are available online)
- Boys Town Social Skill poster, "Using Structured Problem Solving (SODAS)"

TEACHER INSTRUCTIONS:

1. **Prior to class,** locate "Connect the Dots" worksheets on the Internet, print, and have several options available for students.

2. **During class,** distribute one "Connect the Dots" worksheet to each student.

3. Before students begin working on the sheet, ask them what the purpose of a dot-to-dot worksheet is. *(Answer: To connect the dots to make a picture.)* Explain problem-solving is somewhat like a "Connect the Dots" activity because it is necessary to combine all the problem-solving strategies in order to get a "picture" or solution.

4. Allow students to take a few minutes to work on their "Connect the Dots" worksheet.

5. Remind students of the strategies in previous lessons and the Boys Town Social Skill **Using Structured Problem Solving (SODAS):**
   a. *Define the problem Situation.*
   b. *Generate two or more Options.*

      c. *Look at each option's potential Disadvantages.*
      d. *Look at each option's potential Advantages.*
      e. *Decide on the best Solution.*

6. Using scratch paper, ask students to construct a dot-to-dot diagram of strategies used in problem-solving. Provide these instructions:

    a. The first dot should represent the problem and the last dot should be the solution.

    b. They can create an image that represents the solution, or they can make a circular or linear arrangement of dots and label the strategies without creating an image.

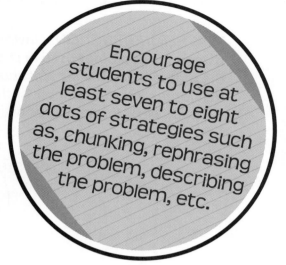

Encourage students to use at least seven to eight dots of strategies such as, chunking, rephrasing the problem, describing the problem, etc.

7. Have students transfer their ideas to a 9" x 12" piece of cardstock and color the dot diagrams.

8. Display the diagrams for visual reminders on the importance of being able to problem solve individually.

9. Before students leave the class, ask them to do a virtual tweet to you, by writing on a piece of paper in 140 characters or less, the importance of being able to solve problems independently. This will allow you to quickly see if any students are struggling with this ability.

ADDITIONAL RESOURCES:
Dot-to-Dot examples to show the students.

Connect the Dots

TEACHER INSTRUCTIONS: Instruct the students to construct a dot-to-dot diagram of strategies used in problem-solving. The first dot should represent the problem and the last dot should be the solution. Students can create an image that represents the solution, or they can make a circular or linear arrangement of dots and label the strategies without creating an image.

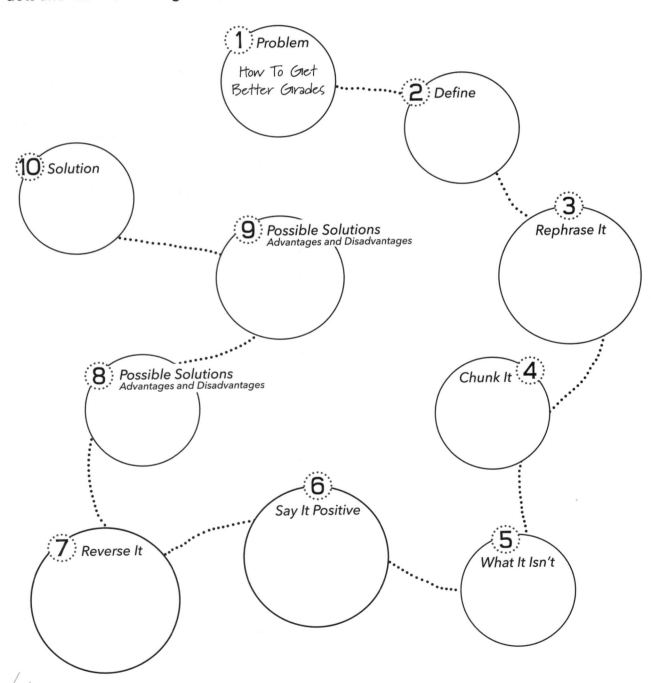

1 Problem
How To Get Better Grades

2 Define

3 Rephrase It

4 Chunk It

5 What It Isn't

6 Say It Positive

7 Reverse It

8 Possible Solutions
Advantages and Disadvantages

9 Possible Solutions
Advantages and Disadvantages

10 Solution

A P P E N D I X

Skills and Their Steps

<u>SECTION 1:</u> *DEFINING AND ADJUSTING*

Sharing Personal Experiences

- Decide if you should share personal experiences with other people.

- Determine whether that person appears comfortable with what you are telling him or her.

- Share experiences that are appropriate for another person to know.

- If what you told the other person is confidential make sure he or she knows that.

Contributing to Discussions

- Look at the person who is talking and wait for a point when no one else is talking.

- Make a short, appropriate comment that relates to the topic being discussed.

- Choose words that are not offensive or confusing to others.

- Give other people a chance to participate.

Identifying Own Feelings

- Examine how you are currently feeling.
- List how your feelings change with different situations and experiences.
- Monitor physical feelings and emotions when actually encountering these situations.
- Correctly identify and label these feelings.
- Communicate these feelings so others can understand them.

Responding to the Feelings of Others

- Listen to the other person.
- Acknowledge what they are saying or writing.
- Express concern or empathy when appropriate.
- Offer to help or provide advice if the other person wants it.
- Encourage the person to seek additional help, if necessary.

Accepting Help or Assistance

- Look at the person offering help.
- Sincerely thank him or her for helping.
- If help is not needed, politely decline the person's assistance.
- If help is needed, accept the help or advice and again thank the person.

Using Structured Problem Solving (SODAS)

- Define the problem or "S"ituation.
- Generate two or more "O"ptions.
- Look at each option's potential "D"isadvantages.
- Look at each option's potential "A"dvantages.
- Decide on the best "S"olution.

Setting Goals

- Decide on your overall values and lifestyle desires.

- List the resources you need to fulfill these lifestyle options.

- Examine the intermediate steps in accomplishing your overall outcome.

- Establish short- and long-term goals that will help you accomplish the steps necessary for the desired outcome.

SECTION 2:   *THE "STINKIN' THINKIN'!"*

Stopping Negative or Harmful Thoughts

- Identify negative or repetitive thoughts you wish to avoid.

- When these occur, consistently say to yourself "Stop!"

- Immediately visualize a more positive scene/statement or relaxing thought.

- Reward yourself for using strategies to stop your negative or harmful thoughts.

Showing Sensitivity to Others

- Express interest and concern for others, especially when they are having trouble or have a bad habit.

- Recognize disabled people deserve the same respect as anyone else.

- Apologize or make amends for hurting someone's feelings or causing harm.

- Recognize people of different races, religions, and backgrounds deserve to be treated the same way as you would expect to be treated.

Choosing Appropriate Words

- Look at the situation and the people around you.

- Know the meanings of words you are about to say/write.

- Refrain from using words that will offend people around you or that they will not understand.

- Avoid using slang, profanity, or words that could have a sexual meaning.

- Decide what thought you want to put into words and then say/write the words.

Analyzing Tasks to Be Completed

- Clarify what task or assignment has been given to you.

- List every step you need to do in order to complete the task.

- Identify which step needs to be done first, second, third, etc.

- Begin completing the steps in order.

SECTION 3: *LET'S GET POSITIVE*

Asking For Help

- Look at the person.
- Ask the person if he or she has time to help you (now or later).
- Clearly describe the problem or what kind of help you need.
- Thank the person for helping you.

Altering One's Environment

- Identify situations in which you encounter difficulty.
- Look for parts of those situations that could be changed to bring about improvement.
- Make appropriate changes to improve self-esteem, behavior, or performance.

Working Independently

- Start on tasks promptly without procrastinating.
- Remain on-task without being reminded.
- Continue working unprompted until the task is completed.
- Check back with the person who assigned the task.

Concentrating on a Subject or Task

- Promptly begin work on the task.
- Focus your attention directly on the subject.
- If your attention wanders, instruct yourself to concentrate on the task.
- Ignore distractions or interruptions by others.
- Remain on-task until the work is completed.

Using Appropriate Humor

- Use humor only under appropriate circumstances.

- Avoid humor that makes fun of groups in society, disabled people, or individuals in your peer group.

- Avoid sexually-oriented jokes and profanity.

- If humor does offend others, be ready to promptly and sincerely apologize.

SECTION 4:   *TURNING PROBLEMS INTO OPPORTUNITIES*

Expressing Optimism

- Look at your group.

- Use an enthusiastic voice tone.

- Describe potential positive outcomes.

- Express hope and desire for positive outcomes.

- Thank the group for listening.

Using Structured Problem Solving (SODAS)

See steps in Section 1

Asking For Clarification

- Look at the person.

- Ask if he or she has time to talk? Don't interrupt.

- Use a pleasant or neutral tone of voice.

- Specifically state what you are confused about. Begin with "I was wondering if…" or "Could I ask about…?"

- Listen to the other person's reply and acknowledge the answer.

- Thank the person for his or her time.

Giving Rationales

- Look at the person in your group.

- Explain your point-of-view with rationales the other person or people can understand.

- Use rationales that point out the potential benefit to the other person(s).

- Ask if the person understands your reasoning.

Doing Good Quality Work

- Find out the exact expectations or instructions for tasks.

- Assemble the necessary tools or materials.

- Carefully begin working. Focus your attention on the task.

- Continue working until the task is completed or criteria are met.

- Examine the results of your work to make sure it was done correctly.

- Correct any deficiencies, if necessary. Perhaps, check back with the person who assigned the task.

Persevering on Tasks and Projects

- Know exactly what must be done in order to complete a task or project.

- Get started promptly without procrastinating.

- Remain on task until finished.

- Deal appropriately with frustrations or disappointments.

SECTION 5: *YOU'VE GOT THIS!*
FROM RESCUE TO PERSONAL AUTONOMY

Dealing with Failure

- Accurately identify you did not succeed in a particular activity.

- Remain calm and relaxed.

- Instruct yourself to control emotional behavior.

- Find a caring adult and discuss your disappointment or other negative feelings.

- Be willing to try again to be successful.

Setting Goals

See steps in Section 2

Choosing Appropriate Words To Say

See steps in Section 1

Using Structured Problem Solving (SODAS)

See steps in Section 1

REFERENCES

https://workinstitute.com/One-Hour-to-Save-the-World

http://www.brainyquote.com/quotes/authors/a/albert_einstein.html

http://www.brainyquote.com/quotes/quotes/h/henryjkai101259.html

http://www.mcescher.com

http://www.merriam-webster.com

http://www.wikihow.com/Pass-Your-Body-Through-a-Sheet-of-Paper

https://www.youtube.com/watch?v=45mMioJ5szc

https://www.youtube.com/watch?v=Oh42WIdyHUw

https://www.youtube.com/watch?v=rGiTDdTC-fY)

https://www.youtube.com/watch?v=t2G8KVzTwfw

Boys Town Press Featured Titles
by Tamara Zentic

978-1-934490-59-4

978-1-934490-83-9

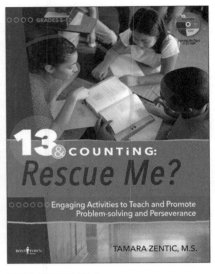

978-1-944882-00-6

978-1-934490-65-5   978-1-934490-64-8

978-1-934490-88-4   978-1-934490-89-1

**For information on Boys Town,
its Education Model®, Common Sense Parenting®,
and training programs:**
boystowntraining.org | boystown.org/parenting
training@BoysTown.org | 1-800-545-5771

**For parenting and educational
books and other resources:**
BoysTownPress.org
EMAIL: btpress@BoysTown.org
PHONE: 1-800-282-6657